ALAN DUKES has worked as an actor with the Sydney Theatre Company, Pork Chop, Griffin, Ensemble, Sydney Symphony Orchestra, Queensland Theatre Company and Riverside Theatre. Alan's stage work includes *The Unlikely Prospect of Happiness*, *Dead Caesar*, *The Great* and *True West* (Sydney Theatre Company); *Shining City* (Inside Job and Griffin Independent); *Alive at Williamstown Pier* (Griffin Theatre); *Mary Stuart* and *Circle Mirror Transformation* (Ensemble); *A Midsummer Nights' Dream* (SSO); *Last Cab to Darwin*, *Ruby's Last Dollar*, *Night of the Sea Monkey* (Pork Chop Productions); as well as performing in his writing debut of *Brilliant Monkey*, for return seasons at the Old Fitzroy and Riverside Theatre and NSW/VIC tour. TV and film credits include: *At Home With Julia*, *Rescue Special Ops*, *East West 101*, *All Saints*, *Rogue Nation*, *Brothers in Arms*, *Devils Dust*, *Beneath Hill 60* and *Redd Inc*.

SEAN RILEY is an award-winning playwright and theatre director based in Adelaide, South Australia. His plays include *Skip Miller's Hit Songs* (Brink Productions, 2011) and *Also a Mirror* (Urban Myth Theatre, 2011), *The Angel and the Red Priest* (Adelaide Festival of the Arts, 2008). For young audiences, *Beautiful Words* (Oddbodies Theatre Company, 2006) won the 2005/06 Adelaide Theatre Guide's Award for Best Dramatic Production, the Adelaide Theatre Critics' Award for Best New Play and the Jill Blewett Playwrights Award (2004). His other work includes *Significant Others* (Oddbodies Theatre Company, 2005), which also was shortlisted for the Patrick White Playwright Award, *The Sad Ballad of Penny Dreadful*, *My Sister Violet*, *The Last Acre* and *The Time of Ashes*.

Brillant Monkey

Alan Dukes

Skip Miller's Hit Songs

Sean Riley

CURRENCY PLAYS

First published in 2012
by Currency Press Pty Ltd,
PO Box 2287, Strawberry Hills, NSW, 2012, Australia
enquiries@currency.com.au
www.currency.com.au

NATIONAL LIBRARY OF AUSTRALIA CIP DATA

Title:	Brilliant monkey & Skip Miller's hit songs / Alan Dukes ; Sean Riley.
ISBN:	9780868199535 (pbk.)
Subjects:	Australian drama—21st century.
Other Authors/Contributors:	
	Dukes, Alan Brilliant monkey.
	Riley, Sean, 1967- Skip Miller's hit songs.
Dewey Number:	A822.4

Contents

Typeset by Claire Grady for Currency Press.
Printed by Hyde Park Press, Richmond, SA.
Front cover shows Warwick Young as Gerard and Alan Dukes as Danny in the
2007 Pork Chop Theatre Company production of *Brilliant Monkey* (photo:
Wendy McDougall); and back cover shows Chris Pitman as Skip Miller in the
2011 Brink production of *Skip Miller's Hit Songs* (photo: Chris Herzfeld).
Cover design by Katy Wall for Currency Press.

Brillant Monkey

Alan Dukes

*Above: Alan Dukes as Danny and Warwick Young as Gerard in the 2007
Pork Chop Theatre Company production at the Old Fitzroy Theatre in
Sydney. Below: Warwick Young as Gerard and Alan Dukes as Danny in the
2007 Pork Chop Theatre Company production at the Old Fitzroy Theatre in
Sydney. (Photos: Wendy McDougall)*

Introduction

It's hard to remember exactly what the genesis for *Brilliant Monkey* was. Alan had taken time out to explore the idea of writing a work for himself, based on stories from his childhood, and Warwick Young was an old mate of his who was about to do a tour of duty in Iraq, but when those first noodles of ideas turned into a 'production' is tough to pinpoint.

My involvement began with Pork Chop Productions, a company that began life as a vehicle to allow myself and friends to produce theatre for mainstream audiences. It was always different to other 'co-op' theatre 'start ups' because (a) it was not a co-op, it was a benevolent dictatorship that aimed to pay everyone professionally; and (b) our productions were staged in large mainstream venues. They took a lot of chutzpah to get up because at the time, and even now, hiring the main stage at Belvoir St was a brash, ambitious and almost impossible thing to do. But we did it. We staged Stoppard's *Rosencrantz and Guildenstern are Dead* to announce ourselves. It was a triumph, and that opening night is still one of my fondest memories.

Soon after I began to encourage friends to submit plays that they had written, or at least discuss ideas they had, in the hope of producing entirely original material. And around the same time, Jeremy Cumpston and his motley crew at Tamarama Rock Surfers grew tired of asking venues to let them stage shows and simply built their own in the cellar at the Old Fitzroy Hotel.

Somewhere in the middle of all this I met a deeply funny, self-effacing young man called Alan, just down from Queensland, whose sense of humour was, tragically, similar to ours, and who, it turned out, was a truly gifted comedic actor. He quickly became part of 'the sty', and I started exploiting his talent for my own selfish needs not long thereafter.

A founding member of Pork Chop was Reg Cribb, and he performed in most of the shows (as a flamenco, synth pop, 80s mime in *R and G* if I remember correctly!). He used to be in rock and roll bands, and most of us thought he had probably done one too many bucket bongs while on the road when he told us he wanted to be a playwright.

Then he dropped a bunch of handwritten pages titled *The Return* on my desk, and I was stunned. It was a proper play. Moving, funny, terrifying and with something to say, The production we mounted for Griffin was a quasi Pork Chop Production and the play really got noticed. It has since been performed all over the world and Reg and I turned it into the feature film *Last Train to Freo* for Pork Chop Productions in 2005.

Reg and I immediately started to think about mounting a large scale, original Australian play. One in the ad hoc style of the company but with bigger ambitions. *Last Cab to Darwin* was the result of that megalomania, and Alan was one of the first people we approached to come and play with us. He created, amongst other things, the all singing all dancing Mayor of Maree 'Ted Mingle', and we were all amazed at his natural gift, not just for performing, but for understanding the structures of a show and judging the right tone. The show, starring Barry Otto and Jackie Weaver, was one of the first co-productions that the Sydney Opera House had attempted. It was a hit.

Alan then starred with Jackie in *Ruby's Last Dollar*, again at the Opera House, and again written by Reg. And again, Alan was brilliant. Around this time he started to discuss the fact that he had been noodling around with the makings of a play himself. I encouraged the idea, and we only had to look to Reg for proof that it really couldn't be *that* hard.

Of course, writing a play is easy. But writing a good one is very, very difficult. I am fairly sure that Alan did a lot of writing and re-writing before he took the plunge and put the dog eared yellow envelope with the words *Brilliant Monkey* scrawled on the front, on my desk .

It was around 2006 when Alan told me that he had organised a staged reading of his new play. I may have sat in on something prior to this, but my memory is of going to the Darlinghurst theatre to see this reading, which had been guided by a couple of old Pork Choppers in Andrew McDonell and Sean Taylor. I was struck by many unexpected aspects of the story, and particularly recognised and enjoyed a signature Pork Chop surrealist style in the occasional 'Major Sneaky Manoeuvre' riffs that dotted the play. Plus it made people laugh, which is always a delight.

Also present at the reading was the elegant Camilla Rowntree, who had just taken a position as a producer at Riverside Theatres in Parramatta. Under the wise and passionate leadership of Robert Love, who I knew well from his time at the Sydney Theatre Company, Riverside had decided to spend some time and money developing and producing new Australian work. They had always been interested in working with Pork Chop, and now we agreed that Alan's play might be the right project to work on together.

We all had a beer, or seven, afterwards and discussed the possibilities. Camilla and Riverside offered us a small grant to allow us to work shop the play out at Parramatta. We accepted, and the team that would guide the show forward was cemented; Alan and Warwick Young, who as an ex-serviceman had been integral to creating the character of Gerard; Andy Macdonell as co-director, Vaike Neeme as Producer and Nicole Robinson as stage manager.

I felt that, given the subject matter, Alan could go further in his exploration of damage and the potential of families to heal. I don't have all the original notes, or even early drafts to fall back on, but I am fairly certain that the idea of Roz, the sister, and the need to go home to Mum's house as a final gesture to work towards was built over the ensuing months as Alan bravely set out to find the most engaging version of the story that he had started to tell.

I often find it difficult to convince writers and creators of the need for sheer bloody-minded hard work: endless redrafting, the ability to listen to criticism and commentary that may not be as constructive as we'd like, the fact that these things never arrive fully formed. In my opinion, *Brilliant Monkey* is being published now because Alan was honest and humble enough to stay open and willing to work towards making a mature, balanced and detailed work. It has never lost its sense of humour or its gentle warmth, but it gained a spine during this process which I think has allowed it to stay lodged in people's memory for longer.

Anyway, the reading we gave after the workshop was less than enthusiastically received. We had pulled the play apart, but hadn't had time to put it all back together again. I struggled to explain that the work we had done in the room was extensive, and would require Alan to go away for a few weeks and just write, in order to make the script work the way we imagined it. Thankfully, Camilla and Robert believed in the work, and we had a co-production partner. The original season would be at the Old Fitzroy, and then we would move out to Riverside once the show was up and running.

The show was an immediate success at the Fitz. People responded so warmly to the mix of simple storytelling, honesty and silliness, that we all felt deeply gratified. Wendy McDougall's photos of that season capture that warmth beautifully. Alan and Warwick are old mates—brothers almost—and their understanding and ease with each other on stage was a big part of the production's attraction to audiences.

The play is about lots of things, but family first and foremost. They are complicated things, and very few of us have them figured out, myself included, but hopefully this play, if you get a chance to see it, or better still, stage it, provides some insights into how central they are to our happiness.

Jeremy Sims,
June 2012
*Jeremy Sims is an actor, director
and founder of Pork Chop Productions.*

Brilliant Monkey was first produced by Pork Chop Productions and Riverside Theatre at The Old Fitzroy Theatre, Woolloomooloo, on 1 April 2007, with the following cast:

GERARD	Warwick Young
DANNY	Alan Dukes

Director, Jeremy Sims
Assistant Director, Andrew McDonell
Designer, Hamish Peters
Lighting Designer, Andrew Williams
Composer, Jed Silver

CHARACTERS

GERARD, 32. A Sergeant in the Australian Army. He is a returned veteran of active service in Afghanistan and has suffered a Traumatic Brain Injury as a result of his proximity to an explosion. He has moved back to his mother's home whilst he is assessed by the military as an outpatient of a repat hospital.

DANNY, 38, Gerard's brother. He is at times homeless and has an ongoing battle with alcohol. He sells the *Big Issue* on the street.

SETTING

The set consists of a park bench, an overhanging tree branch and a working door.

The play is set in several locations delineated by different lighting states. A park close to the city, a busy city street, and outside their mother's inner suburban house. The Sneaky Manoeuvres were performed in spotlight in the first production.

ACKNOWLEDGEMENTS

This play would not have been possible without the help of Jeremy Sims, Vaike Neeme, Wendy McDougall, Andrew McDonell, Nicole Robinson, Paul Daley, Warwick Young, Glenn Terry, Robert Love, Camilla Rountree, Sean Taylor, Melanie de Ferranti and the serving and returned service personnel of the Australian Army.

SCENE ONE

The park. An Australian soldier, GERARD, *on a bench. He seems agitated. He holds a peeled banana and is about to take a bite but becomes disinterested and places it on the bench.*

SCENE TWO

The park. Later. A homeless man, DANNY, *on the same bench. He sees the half-eaten banana, looks around, takes the banana, turns it upside down in its skin and eats what is left.*

SCENE THREE

The park. The sound of excited military radio traffic; voices relay coordinates and orders. The sound of artillery escalates to a terrific explosion.

GERARD, *dressed in army uniform, is asleep on a park bench.* DANNY *enters and freezes upon seeing the sleeping soldier. He slowly edges around* GERARD *and reaches out to tap his shoulder.* GERARD *wakes instantly, punching* DANNY, *and immediately has him pinned on the ground.*

GERARD: Righto, what's your fucking game!?
DANNY: My ear! I can't—
GERARD: Answer me!
DANNY: I'm bleeding—
GERARD: You are not... Fucking hell! Dan... Danny is that you? Where did you come from? Jesus, I'm sorry—
DANNY: You're sorry—
GERARD: You okay? Don't wake me up like that, for Christ's sake! Just shake my boot or—
DANNY: I shake your boot you'd have kicked me in the frigging head. Who wakes someone up like that?
GERARD: [*calling to unseen onlookers*] It's okay! It's, family!

DANNY: My neck hurts. My ear feels like a pikelet.

GERARD: Sit down.

DANNY: No. I'm fine.

GERARD *stands back and looks* DANNY *up and down.*

GERARD: Well… Shit.

DANNY: Yeah I know.

GERARD: Eh?

DANNY: That's the smell. I've got shit on me from the zoo.

GERARD: Huh?

DANNY: I thought that's what you meant—

GERARD: What?

DANNY: —when you said shit.

GERARD: No. I mean look at you.

DANNY: Sunday best.

GERARD: Must've been a prick of a week.

DANNY *starts to walk away.*

DANNY: Tell Mum I saw you. Should do this again.

GERARD: Danny! Hang on. Wait up… I got a shock.

DANNY: Was that it was it? [*Pause.*] When did you get back?

GERARD: Don't you talk to Mum?

DANNY: No.

GERARD: You should talk to Mum.

DANNY: Roz told me you were here.

GERARD: Still keeping in touch with Sis?

DANNY: She… I… Still got all your arms and legs? I was going to send a card.

GERARD: Too late.

DANNY: Right. [*Pause.*] Roz said something big went off over there. I said whatever it was it probably knocked some sense into you.

GERARD: Did ya?

DANNY: Y'know, about getting out of the army before you really—

GERARD: I'm not getting out of the army—

DANNY: That's what she said. I guess you're heading back up north soon?

GERARD: Staying with Mum until I sort some stuff out. Army stuff.

DANNY: Closest I've been back home is getting hit in the head with a bottle of Bundy.

GERARD: Eh?

DANNY: I've been hit in the head with a bottle before, Chicken Tonight jar, makes a very distinct echo—

GERARD: Dan—

DANNY: And a spade, and a baseball bat, right here in this park.

GERARD: You've been hit a lot?

DANNY: Well that all happened on the same day.

GERARD: Sit down.

DANNY: No. [*Pause.*] You look good.

GERARD: Yeah. Fuck me eh? That's what…?

DANNY: I dunno… ten—

GERARD: Ten years. Bloody hell. Blink and you miss it. Well … What's ahh… Where you living? Mum wasn't sure.

DANNY: Oh I've got a cracker of a place. Yeah, a real nice joint. Overlooks a park down here… I'm in sales now.

GERARD: Fuck eh? Where?

DANNY: Wherever it takes me.

GERARD: Who for?

DANNY: A magazine. You probably wouldn't know it.

GERARD: Any good at it?

DANNY: Yeah. I'm new at it but… people are buying and there's the odd smile.

GERARD: Smiling people aren't always a good sign.

DANNY: Sometimes you get the cork eye, but I always liked being looked at.

GERARD: Well that's good… Do you need some coin? What do you need?

DANNY: No I'm fine.

GERARD: Yeah.

DANNY: I come through here. How long—

GERARD: All week. I'm having some tests done at the hospital. Fuck. Danny. Come back to Mum's. I'll be free in an hour.

DANNY: You know the rules. No animals in the house.

SCENE FOUR

A street. Dan stands alone on his pitch. He holds the Big Issue *magazine and spruiks. He talks to an unseen passerby.*

DANNY: *The Big Issue.* Five Dollars. Five dollars is all. Thanks Michael. Have a good day eh? Good sorts around today, eh Michael? There was a time when they would have looked at me...

He addresses the audience.

I can't recall the year but I was definitely younger, well, *Xanadu* was the hottest ticket in town. I'm in this town with twenty-one thousand other Queenslanders and... Felicia Van Lathen. Felicia was a very attractive girl, a figure honed by hours of netball, greeny green eyes and a laugh that gently rang the bell. She was, as some of the kids would say 'the duck's nuts'. I never told her that.

I was a wiry, sandy haired kid with a cowlick and buck teeth like 'Bucky Beaver' and to really arse things up I was in some kind of love with Felicia Van Lathen.

I can't recall the month but it was hot, bloody bastard hot. I would bike down to the big park and watch umpteen games of netball, just so I might bump into Felicia at the soft drink caravan. I would take enough money for two cans of Sunshine Pine, just in case I had to hang around for a while.

I can't recall the day but there was definitely netball being played and I bumped into Felicia at the soft drink caravan and I buy her a can of Sunshine Pine, and just as I'm flashing the bucks around I decided to ask her to go with me and she said where? I panicked and said *Xanadu*, the hottest ticket in town or so they said... and for some reason she said yes.

I can't recall the hour but it was dark and I met Felicia with two tickets, my new Glow-weave shirt and a smile you couldn't knock off, even though I knew I wouldn't be able to kiss her without loosening a few of her teeth. I really just wanted to sit next to her for a while. The hairs on my arm stood on end, I was gone.

I can't recall the minute, but I crept my arm around her shoulder and kissed her on the neck, which she seemed to like. I was hovering above the seat, giddy from the hypnotic effect of the soundtrack.

I can however recall the second. Halfway through Gene Kelly's roller skating number I laughed and farted at the same time. A loud laugh, and an equally loud fart. Kids could tell where it came from even in the dark. Felicia didn't look at me, just got up and moved. Felicia Van Lathen never went with me anywhere, anymore after that. Life changes in an instant eh? Success always occurs in private and failure… in full fucking view.

He goes back to spruiking.

Big Issue!

SCENE FIVE

A ferry terminal. GERARD *enters a ferry terminal, checks the indicator board, places his shopping bag on the bench and sits down. He addresses the audience.*

GERARD: Mum never really pushed me into going into the army. I was always a kid who was in the cadets, air training corps, those types of groups y'know and I guess I'd really wanted to have a sense of purpose. My dad died and my brother left home early. I wasn't getting it trying for a trade. I wasn't getting it working with some of the people that I was working with, and when I joined the army, I got that… I got that. I want to go back. I'm a sergeant so I've got responsibilities, but at the moment… I'd go back tomorrow if I could. I'd do that. I've been home close to six months now. Two in hospital. Two in rehab, and back with the unit up in Townsville, which wasn't working. Now I'm back here… I'm not sure what's going to happen. My injury's been classed as minor. At the moment I'm just looking forward to Anzac day on Friday and being able to ride in the car again without feeling sick.

He rises to look at the indicator board and is distracted by the announcement.

VOICEOVER: Sydney Ferries are co-operating the Governments Counter Terrorism Initiative. If you see an unattended package or someone behaving suspiciously tell a crew member or alert the police.

GERARD *looks around and fails to recognise his shopping bag.*

He becomes extremely agitated.

GERARD: Whose is that!? Whose bag is that!? It's not funny!

    GERARD *realises his mistake. He addresses the audience.*

It's mine.

SCENE SIX

Spotlight up on a highly-strung officer, the MAJOR, *standing very close to* CORPORAL *who is standing to attention.*

MAJOR: Corporal at ease. Major Sneaky Manoeuvre. Good News. Today a manoeuvre so Machiavellian in its intent, so deceptive in its purpose, it will catalyse you into the disquieting world of the ignoramus and keep you busier than a one-eyed man in a strip joint. The details could not fill the back of a sequin, yet this hag's mash of unrest will leave you unable to even finger-paint the experience.

CORPORAL: Yes Sir!

MAJOR: North Korea's President has accused our Prime Minister of killing a baboon and stealing its face. This is the last straw.

    Using the same raw materials as that of Icarus, you will attempt a flyover of Kim Jong Un's thirtieth Birthday party in Pyong Yang later this afternoon and during the raising of the flags' ceremony attempt to replace the North Korean Flag with a pair of John Galliano's pants.

CORPORAL: Expensive Sir.

MAJOR: This is war man! By midday you'll have been aloft for three hours depending on thermals and luck. When you sense Jong Un is about to open his presents you are to swoop low, corkscrewing through the assembled throng and make the swap. Down comes the flag on go the pants. National embarrassment. Regime change.

CORPORAL: And the hard part Sir?

MAJOR: Now the hard part. Jong Un is very quick over short distances as well as being fuelled by an intense reactive suspicion of flight. At no stage allow him to get you on the ground as wax and feathers tend to make a fist fight clownish... and Corporal?

CORPORAL: Yes Sir.

MAJOR: Don't answer the door to Dr Cock-up. Dismissed.

SCENE SEVEN

The park. DANNY *sits on the bench reading the* Big Issue. *He is startled by a quietly approaching* GERARD.

DANNY: Shit!

GERARD: What are you reading?

DANNY: The *Big Issue*. The finance section. You want to read it?

GERARD: Got plenty of other things to occupy me.

> *Pause.*

DANNY: You're shaking.

GERARD: Must've pinched a nerve.

DANNY: You reckon?

> DANNY *notices a bird.*

WAGTAIL... they'll go just about anything.

> DANNY *sees another.*

RED Wattle bird, beautiful.

> GERARD *pays no attention and stares at his trembling hand.* DANNY *attempts to distract his brother.*

Tawny Frogmouth, strange, nocturnal. Cassowary. Normally only see them at the zoo... Hey Gerard. What's your favourite animal?

GERARD: Beef.

DANNY: I meant—

GERARD: Or Rabbit, yeah yeah. We had one for an escape and evasion exercise.

DANNY: Eh?

GERARD: Survival behind enemy lines. My patrol was given a ahh... rabbit to keep safe. We had to keep the thing hidden and bring it back alive.

DANNY: Did you?

GERARD: Well that was the objective.

DANNY: Good.

GERARD: Grew quite attached to it. The boys that had the chicken didn't do as well though.

DANNY: Did they lose it?

GERARD: Kinda.

DANNY: Oh… I carried a raw egg around in my pocket for two days but never got to cook it, got crushed on the 423. What'd you eat?

GERARD: Can't tell you.

DANNY: What? National security? What if I get lost and need food?

GERARD: In the park?

DANNY: Fair call.

GERARD: You wouldn't know hungry.

DANNY: Yeah I fucking would.

GERARD: No you wouldn't, not here. We were holding a position just outside the village of… Khost and we see some Northern Alliance soldiers running across this field under heavy fire. They're ducking and weaving like cut cats, trying to get over to their mates. They've got machine guns and RPG's strapped to their backs but they're all carrying something in their hands, no one could make it out. Maybe explosives. When they finally get under cover of the incline they put their weapons down and really carefully unwrap these packages. And… What is it?

DANNY: I don't know.

GERARD: It's bread. Under fire and they're carrying bread.

I think I said to Kenny. Don't think I'm going to put my arse on the line to get you your brekkie—

DANNY: Yeah right—

GERARD: That was a joke. Anyway the enemy were still banging away at us with all they got until this AC-130 was brought in to y'know… air-condition them.

Pause.

DANNY: I'm glad you're back in one piece, Gerard.

GERARD: Everyone expects you to come home, don't they?

DANNY: They expect you to, yes. They want you back the same.

GERARD: Nothing's ever the same. You learn that.

DANNY: You must be heading back soon.

GERARD: Where?

DANNY: Your base. Townsville.

GERARD: I can't fly just yet. [*He points to his head.*] I'm staying for the march and we'll see how things go from there. It'd be good if you could poke your head in at home too, Danny. This has got to fucking stop. Mum hasn't said as much but I know she worries herself sick.

DANNY: I'll call.

GERARD: Why not come over for fuck's sake?

DANNY: How about Friday?

GERARD: That's fucking Anzac Day.

DANNY: Bugger. Thursday I'm at the zoo. I could…

GERARD: Don't bother.

SCENE EIGHT

The street. DANNY *stands on his pitch and addresses unseen passers-by.*

DANNY: *Big Issue*! Back to school special! Four bucks! C'mon kids, cheaper than a pen.

DANNY *watches them walk on. He addresses the audience.*

Some days after little school, primary school Roz would have her friends over and she would make me hang from our trees for her backyard zoo tours, and they would be shown my mango throwing monkey or my wounded Ibis that lived on the compost heap. I could do about twenty animals. Sometimes she would sit me in pretend school classes under our house and I'd be labelled 'Troublemaker' without even having done anything. Everyone else was a doll and she was the teacher. She would leave the dolls and I in the classroom, when she was called away and then storm back in and demand to know who had been talking. I knew she was gunning for me but I would panic and point at one or two of the dolls or the Gollywog. Which were thrashed like stink and dragged by whatever limb was still attached out of the room to a pretty grisly end I used to think. The rest of us would keep pretty quiet after that but I could feel the stares as if I had betrayed them, and I had. She was a funny kid. I rarely ask her but she'll help me out if… well she's the eldest so it comes with the territory, doesn't it? Sense of responsibility. After Dad went someone had to step up. She takes care of anything Mum needs, but I can tell it shits her. I'd help but she stopped asking a while ago. Probably thought I'd drink the milk money. Mum once told me I had a heart of gold, but y'know so does a boiled egg. *Big Issue*!

SCENE NINE

The park. GERARD *is seated on the park bench. He has a headache.* DANNY *paces with a crossword.*

DANNY: G hour?

GERARD: Huh?

DANNY: G hour. Could that be some military term?

GERARD: No.

DANNY: Like Guard hour?

GERARD: Guard Hour?

DANNY: Yeah.

GERARD: No.

DANNY: Like alpha foxhole zeppity.

GERARD: Yeah. No.

DANNY: What's G?

GERARD: I've got a fucking… breezeblock in my head Dan. So don't start.

DANNY: It's probably Gamma. Or Gretel. Garbo. 'Alpha Garbo. Alpha Garbo this is Orange Fanta come back.'

GERARD: Alpha, Bravo, Charlie… Alpha, Bravo, Charlie…

DANNY: Doesn't matter.

GERARD: What's this for?

DANNY: Cryptic. Keeps your noggin sharp. You should try it.

GERARD *throws a bottle top and hits him.*

Midnight. G hour, middle letter in night is G. G hour. Midnight. [*He points to his head.*] Alert. Y'know when I copped that flogging I thought I was the unluckiest fella around.

GERARD: You were asleep in a park.

DANNY: Playground.

GERARD: Playground. You think you'd be safe. Roz told me. She looked after you.

DANNY: Of course.

GERARD: Why'd they pick you?

DANNY: Sleeping rough. It's a lottery isn't it? Random.

GERARD: If you ever see those kids again give me the nod.

DANNY: They weren't kids. They certainly weren't kids… Anyway in hospital I found I could get a few of these cryptics. Beats me. I started writing little bits and pieces too. Things I see and feel. I make up poems when I'm on my pitch. I'm going to get them put in the mag. That's my dream anyway and they pay the contributors.

GERARD: Writing poems?

DANNY: Yeah I love it. I can't help it. You ever tried?

GERARD: Could do it with my prick out. Got a million.

> There once was a scientist named Lil.
> Took a chance on a Nuclear Pill.
> They found her vagina
> In South Carolina—

DANNY: I don't know that one.

GERARD: What the fuck is it?

DANNY: It's not a poem.

GERARD: They found her vagina in South Carolina … they found her vagina in South Carolina…

DANNY: Something that rhymes with pill?

GERARD: Well go on, smart arse, let's hear one of your pearls.

DANNY: You want to hear one? Sure.

> I loved to touch you,
> The outline of your body,
> That unsteady capture of something brilliant.
> The keen fragrances you gave,
> The kisses of pelting rain.

> GERARD *laughs.*

GERARD: Who's that about?

DANNY: Doesn't matter.

SCENE TEN

The park. GERARD *stands looking out across the park.* DANNY *enters with two Heinekens.*

DANNY: Hey buggerlugs! Thought you might be keen for a drink. Hey? Swapped 'em for a mag.

> *He presents the two beers.* GERARD *can't decide.*

Take that cause this one's meiniken.

GERARD: You drinking?

DANNY: I'm celebrating your return. Anyway we're at war. If we don't drink they win. You're early.

GERARD: No. No. I ahh… Can't sit in that waiting room. Too much action. They usually give me a call when I'm next and I walk up the hill.

DANNY: You busy?

GERARD: Busy trying to get some action on my case. Giving me the shits. You'd think I was trying to stiff them.

DANNY: You're not are you?

GERARD: No. The results are coming back negative but I'm still walking into things. It's all light and noise. I can't taste anything so something's wrong. All they do is adjust some meds, tell me to lose weight, get more exercise. Maybe I should join a fucking mixed netball comp or get some mates together for Skirmish…

I'm dealing with different departments. I'm always losing my rag cause I got to tell the story over and over again… I'd prefer to stay at home.

Gerard looks down at his beer.

What are you doing, Dan? I can't drink this! I've got the dawn service coming up on Friday. I'm still feeling groggy. I don't want to career off into the crowd.

DANNY: If you're dizzy you shouldn't be marching.

GERARD: Fuck that! I'm not missing that march. Someone's picking me up. Some fella from the RSL.

DANNY: Oh yeah who's that?

GERARD: I… what does it matter?

DANNY: It doesn't.

GERARD: You wouldn't know him.

DANNY: The unknown soldier?

GERARD: [*flaring in anger at* DANNY] Not funny.

DANNY: You know you haven't told me what happened.

GERARD: It was a pressure wave from the explosion.

DANNY: Good. Keep it simple.

GERARD: Affected the right side.

He points to his left side of his head.

DANNY: Because you were closest to the blast?

GERARD: That's what the report says. I'm pretty sure there were others closer.

DANNY: Lucky.

GERARD: Was I? I remember being in Kandahar. In a marketplace. I was… using an interpreter to talk to a local fella and his son, gathering intelligence. From what they tell me someone's strapped a load of bang to a donkey somewhere nearby in the crowd. They used to use cars and bikes but we were awake to that, so now they use these little donkeys…

DANNY: You didn't kill it, did you?

GERARD: There's so many of them. Everywhere—

DANNY: Probably bad luck killing a donkey—

GERARD: And when this donkey's gone up it's wiped out everyone around it. This father and son's copped the whole box and dice. Cleaned 'em all up. If we'd have been standing any other way.

DANNY: How are those headaches?

GERARD: One's floating around up there. It'll come on later, always does.

DANNY: Do you know what you're going to do?

GERARD: Well sometimes I don't know whether I want a shit or a haircut so it's hard to know, but if I'm a slower thinker now I must have been quick.

DANNY: Should've been a stand-up.

GERARD: Hey, haven't told you this one. Journo's done a story on Afghanistan before the War, and he's noticed back then that the wives always walked behind their husbands.

DANNY: Ah…

GERARD: You heard it? Anyway he's gone back to… to Afghanistan and noticed that now the wives walk in front of their husbands and he's gone up to one of the women and asked what's caused it? And she's said…

DANNY & GERARD: [*together*] Land mines.

DANNY: You should get up there. Keep your appointment.

> GERARD *goes to exit.*

Maybe you can come into town soon see me weave my magic.

GERARD: Can't be Wednesday, I got the march… and I expect to see you there, Danny. For Grandad at least.

SCENE ELEVEN

Mum's house. GERARD *storms out the door of his mothers house cursing. He takes a moment to calm down and rests on his haunches.*

GERARD: There was a bloke that lived up the road from us as kids. Old guy. He'd walk past our place and he'd always stop and stare at something on the ground, wouldn't take his eyes of it. Then he'd back up and walk around it and keep going until he saw it again. There was nothing there. Dad said he'd served in North Africa and he thought they were land mines. Land mines on Fort Street. That would've made Red Rover fun. When the show was in town he'd disappear cause of the fireworks. I used to find it piss funny. Grandad served. 53rd Battalion 5th Division. Fromelles. Saw action then went AWOL four times, mostly in France. Love to know what he got up to. Wasn't long after that he got gassed, sent home. Slowly drank himself to death. I'll be marching for him on Wednesday and for my mates and the landmine guy. I'll head back inside soon. Giving them a break. Roz doesn't like being around me too much. I guess I'm used to doing things a certain way. She reckons I'm swearing and carrying on which upsets Mum but… half the time I don't remember so I've got to keep my mouth shut. I mean I couldn't tell you what I told the doctor yesterday. He'll read me back what he's written down but I don't remember saying it so I tend to clam up which causes problems later. I just feel… different.

SCENE TWELVE

Spotlight up on the CORPORAL *standing at attention.*

MAJOR: Corporal. At ease. Major Sneaky Manoeuvre. Good news. Today you will mount up and canter into the gaping maw of hell. You are to undertake a mission so dangerous only the condemned would consider.

CORPORAL: Yes Sir.

MAJOR: This blind date with lunacy requires the cunning of the disenfranchised, and the mercy of the airborne virus. But of course you don't tell the men.

CORPORAL: No Sir.

MAJOR: ASIO has made it quite clear to us that the head of al Qaeda, Ayman al-Zawahiri is at present hiding in the quaint villages of South Australia, possibly working for one of the local trade guilds in the lead up to their biggest cultural event of the year. We believe his next target to be the Maypoles of Hahndorf.

CORPORAL: The cheeky fuck Sir.

MAJOR: Cheeky fuck Corporal. Your training should tell you the natural enemy of the Egyptian terrorist is of course the three-inch mortar.

CORPORAL: Permission to use the leg of a Steinway Sir.

MAJOR: Very good. Can't be giving you all the froo froo. Now, dressed as teenage Fräuleins, your first objective is to locate al-Zawahiri, and with your attractively unfamiliar German charm, persuade him to bang the local schnapps down until he's as drunk as a fresh boiled owl. The fact that he's a committed teetotaller could make this a real poser.

CORPORAL: And the hard part Sir?

MAJOR: Now the hard part. The last thing this devout Muslim will be expecting whilst in hiding is to be converted to Lutheran. This would normally be a solemn ceremony involving the reading of the Augsburg confession of 1530 and a lot of candles. Time restraints and no clear protocol means going at him like stink with the piano leg until you are convinced he has embraced all aspects of the Lutheran ideal.

CORPORAL: Understood Sir.

MAJOR: After that the Coalition requests you send him to that dark place to join the earth unnoticed... and Corporal.

CORPORAL: Sir?

MAJOR: Lets not get sand in the vas. Dismissed.

Spotlight out.

SCENE THIRTEEN

The park. DANNY *and* GERARD *are watching an event. The happy sounds of it filter in.*

DANNY: Looks like that rain coming might spoil the… [*He peers into the distance and reads a banner.*] Global Peace…

DANNY & GERARD: [*together*] Meditation Day.

DANNY: Crazy Castle. No rides though. Should I go see if they've got any coconut-ice? Not like the Maryborough Show.

GERARD *does not respond*

I'd like to get back up to Maryborough one day, wouldn't you?

GERARD: No.

DANNY: See what's changed. What pubs are still open. Got to be some shut eh? Twenty-six for twenty odd thousand people. Madness. Check out the Mary at high tide. Go for a swim.

GERARD: Stains your skin.

DANNY: Yeah. Wonder we never drowned. Like that Cooper kid.

GERARD: Who?

DANNY: Who? He was one of your mates.

GERARD: I… I had a lot of mates.

DANNY: Sure. But you used to have him round all the time.

GERARD: What was his name?

DANNY: Someone Cooper.

GERARD: What'd he look like?

DANNY: Poor and sweaty… I don't know. When they found him he didn't have a head.

GERARD: We had lots of kids over.

DANNY: Not headless ones… You were always into guns. I gave you your first gun.

GERARD: Yeah.

DANNY: A little Czech air rifle.

GERARD: That's right.

DANNY: I reckon we almost stopped the Cane toad in its tracks with one air rifle… and a hockey stick. I remember pinging a red belly black… lots under the old corro… I didn't want to but Dad said there's just so many of them they'll get in the house.

GERARD: How are you fairing Dan?

DANNY: I'm fine. You're the worry, I mean you'll tell me one thing one day and out the other.

GERARD: Eh?

DANNY: Gerard, I've got to tell you something about Dad.

GERARD: Not another poem. I'm not one hundred per cent.

DANNY: It's not a poem.

GERARD: Well?

DANNY: Nuh. Gone. Hey, yeah. Remember that fight I had with Martin someone at school?

GERARD: Oh yeah.

DANNY: You weren't there yet. He was smaller than me but he picked it, anyway I've caned him, and fuck, didn't fight news travel fast. All his mates were scouring the school for me until Rodney Tunks got me on the way to umm... Tech drawing.

GERARD: Ambushed you.

DANNY: Yeah. Tunksy's waltzed up to me. He was a big tall prick remember. Punched me like fuck fair in the friggin ear. So hard that I pissed meself... which isn't cool... but it's the shock of it eh? He was biting his lip as he hit me. Never forget that look. Ever been punched in the ear?

GERARD: Nah. Too quick. Did you punch him back?

DANNY: No I went home, I mean you can't go to tech drawing with pissed pants, can ya?

> DANNY *picks up a piece of wood and moves to* GERARD.

GERARD: What are you doing?

DANNY: Just showing you something. That's when we were living in Lennox Street remember?

GERARD: Fibro place.

DANNY: Weatherboard. Across from the bike racks. I got out your air rifle that I'd scoped in the day before, sat at the bedroom window and waited for the prick. [*He raises the wood as a gun*] Thought about... shooting him and the deal with all that... then I saw him laughing and muscling his way out of the gates on his new ten-speed and in those crosshairs for a brief second was his ugly bullet bait nut, I really wanted him... I dunno dead or blind.

GERARD: Jesus. You're a fucking psycho.

DANNY: He was trying to do a wheelie and the slugs smacked fair into his left foot, brought him off squealing like a stuck pig. Didn't know what the fuck had happened. Blaming everyone.

GERARD: You shot him?

DANNY: Not dead. In the shoe. With a pellet.

GERARD: You shot him?!

DANNY: Never told you that. Should have just listened to Dad eh? If they're smaller than you punch them in the head. If they're bigger than you—

GERARD: Punch them in the throat. I wish he was still around.

DANNY: Yeah. That would have changed things. Gerard? You ever kept a secret for so long you wonder if it ever happened?

GERARD: I don't have secrets.

DANNY: No. Hey, Tunksy never worked it out eh. Went on to work in local tourism I think. Got away with it. The one slug theory. He deserved it. Even Stevens.

GERARD: Fairs fair. You smell that?

DANNY: No.

GERARD: Like… like brakes.

> *The sound of a carnival filters in.* DANNY *starts dancing to it. Unbeknownst to* DANNY, GERARD *suffers a small seizure and his arm begins to flap uncontrollably.*

SCENE FOURTEEN

The park. GERARD *is seated on a park bench. He stares into the ground.* DANNY *stands close by and stares at some leaf litter. He picks out a take-away coffee lid, attaches it to his ear and looks over to* GERARD *with mock exasperation.*

DANNY: Alright! Who threw that?

> *Silence.* DANNY *picks up a paper bag.*

Remember this?

> *He throws an invisible ball in the air and pretends to catch it, clicking his fingers on the bag to imitate the sound of the ball*

dropping in. GERARD *watches him in silence. He then throws the invisible ball to* GERARD. GERARD *throws the invisible ball away.* DANNY *still pretends to catch it.*

World's a funny place isn't it?

GERARD: Don't start.

DANNY: Jeff one of the other sellers was telling me. He was sitting having a beer in the Criterion the other day—

GERARD: Can I have some peace and quiet?

DANNY: Well you're in the right place. Anyway he could hear this fella, singing out and talking to himself and when he walks past Jeff to go to the dunny he hits him on the neck *Coonk.* 'That's a karate chop from Korea'—

GERARD: You're fulla shit—

DANNY: No-one sees it and Jeff's going fucking whoa, you know. He picks himself up but he reckons when this fella walks by on the way back he hits Jeff on the other side of the neck *Fung* and says 'That's a judo chop from Japan'.

So Jeff's had enough, y'know, no-ones seeing him getting clobbered so he doesn't hang around but about half an hour later he's back and sees this prick still playing the slots and he walks up behind him, smacks him in the head and knocks him out and Jeff says to the barman, 'When he wakes up, tell him that was a fuckin' crowbar from Bunnings'.

GERARD: Is that for real?

DANNY: Yeah.

GERARD: You sure?

DANNY: What are you saying? I don't have any mates?

SCENE FIFTEEN

The park. DANNY *is seated.* GERARD *paces.*

GERARD: There were times when we would go out to ahh…

DANNY: Teddington Weir?

GERARD: No.

DANNY: The pontoon?

GERARD: No. Listen. Out at—

DANNY: Did you ride there?

GERARD: Yes.

DANNY: Wasn't the pontoon then.

GERARD: No.

DANNY: Cos you could only walk. Showgrounds?

GERARD: No.

DANNY: That's been pulled down.

GERARD: I know.

DANNY: Couldn't have cos that's only been recently.

GERARD: The bridge.

DANNY: Lamington?

GERARD: Lamington bridge.

DANNY: What'd you do?

GERARD: Lots of stuff.

DANNY: Fishing. Mangrove jacks, flatties.

GERARD: Yeah.

DANNY: Catfish. We'd throw them under the semi-trailers remember?

GERARD: Yep.

DANNY: Used to tell you their spikes would puncture the tyres. You used to bomb off it.

GERARD: Yeah, bombing.

DANNY: Maybe we should go back up there?

GERARD: No-one's there anymore.

DANNY: Blacky's still up there.

GERARD: Fuck Blacky.

DANNY: Yeah. Fuck Blacky.

GERARD: I miss 'em.

DANNY: We should go back.

GERARD: Not them, my mates.

DANNY: Have you heard from them?

GERARD: Sometimes you think they've forgotten you—

DANNY: Forgotten or you've disappeared.

GERARD: You wonder—

DANNY: You do—

GERARD: What they're doing. If they talk about you—

DANNY: Talking's good—

GERARD: You don't think you'd miss 'em—

DANNY: No good keeping it in—

GERARD: Sometimes it's hard to remember them as a group—

DANNY: Monkeys live in groups.

GERARD: Fuck monkeys!

DANNY: Why would you say that?!

GERARD: Fuck em and burn em!

DANNY: Army's made you nasty. Eh? Can't we leave anything alone? Not even the brilliant monkeys? Gentle apes.

GERARD: Don't start.

DANNY: I was reading about this gorilla called Michael that's learnt sign language.

GERARD: That's right. Nothing to say so you say it.

DANNY: I should take you to the zoo. Young girl there let's me in for a mag. Show you the monkeys, the gorillas, see how they get on. They'll look at you without judgement, they grunt. They acknowledge you. I don't spend time with any other animals—

GERARD: I should get going …

DANNY: Sometimes the seals. I heard this guy saved a little gibbon from being eaten by chimps. Put his life in danger to rescue her. When they asked him why he said when he looked into her eyes he didn't think twice. You just have to look into their eyes and you can see what he meant. Have you ever done that? Looked into their eyes?

GERARD: Yeah… Donkey Kong.

A long pause.

DANNY: Well you haven't got much to laugh about so it's good you're laughing.

GERARD: Hey! This is the first time today I haven't had a fucking headache. It's not much fun hanging around your sorry guts either. And maybe you should try having a tub.

DANNY: Some guy was passed out in the bathroom this morning.

GERARD: Where do you live Danny? Eh? I've seen you sleeping down here.

DANNY: Old habits. I do it to be able to catch up with you.

GERARD: Well don't bother if you're just going to fucking blather on.

DANNY: I was talking about something.

GERARD: *I was talking about something!*

DANNY: I heard you. I always hear you. It's not all about you little brother.

GERARD: *It's not all about me? When has it ever been about fucking me?! Jesus, I could just fucking…* Y'know when you left home I reckon I stopped growing for a year. You brushed me. I'd planned all this stuff we were going to do, but getting fucked up was a bit higher on the list eh?

DANNY: That wasn't it Gerard.

GERARD: I trawl over our time together. Had I said something? Had I done something? I couldn't tell. It's still a fucking mystery to me and y'know, I don't want an answer. I don't know how Roz speaks to you, what you've put her through, all her plans changed. But you know what? In the end… I didn't want to end up like you. Just fucking vanished. You're… oh forget it.

DANNY: I'm what?

GERARD: [*pointing at him*] *You're this!*

> *Silence, then quietly.*

DANNY: My name is Danny. I'm remembering your life for you. It's not all good. We lost our Dad.

GERARD: Well I remember that fucking much!

SCENE SIXTEEN

The street. DANNY *stands on his pitch. He has no magazines. He has been drinking and is singing a Billy Joel song.*

DANNY: Sputnik choeylie something on the river Kwai. 'Homicide. Children of Thalidomide'. Four Dollars. The *Big Issue*!

> DANNY *notices a beggar. The beggar's replies are implied but not heard.*

Hey mate don't beg here, this my pitch… for a fucking long time. I'm working for a living. I'm not a beggar I'm not begging. I can stand on my own two feet, everyone's on eye level and I'm not some piece of shit that you can scrape off the bottom of your shoe, Gerard! Murderer! I'm not talking to you. Well that's fucking charming… aren't you a fucking charmer hey? Mum would be proud! *Don't give to this prick! He could make an effort! Even your sign's fucked!*

Big Issue! Read the mag. I'll be in it soon. I'm writing. My words. [DANNY *looks at the buyer's nametag.*] Gary. I used to know a Gary. Dead now. Flipped off the front of a 4WD and it run him… Well you have a fuck'n good day Gary! [*Hisses to beggar.*] Cunt.

SCENE SEVENTEEN

The park. GERARD *is seated.* DANNY *enters.*

DANNY: Been at the zoo. Wrong time of day, everyone's asleep. Anyway sorry.

GERARD: Sorry for what?

DANNY: Sorry for what? Sorry for what you said.

GERARD: What? About Monkeys?

DANNY: I… people… tourists. The amount of lost kids at Central. I take them straight to the transits.

GERARD: Danny.

DANNY: I still take part in everything.

GERARD: What are you going on…?

DANNY: You said I was [*referring to himself*]… this.

GERARD: This what?

DANNY: Dunno. Do you want to hear the hundred I came up with?

GERARD: Oh put down the rum brother. When did I say that? You're losing it.

DANNY: Do you think I'm drunk? I don't drink but for special occasions.

GERARD: You sure? I can smell it on you.

DANNY: That's Listerine.

GERARD: You're not drinking that shit!? [*Pause.*] I'm a cranky prick sometimes.

DANNY: Yeah.

GERARD: My brain got knocked around, so it's going to take—

DANNY: Forever—

GERARD: A while for everything to settle back into place… my head's—

DANNY: You're in a bit of strife—

GERARD: Like a ball of aching cotton wool.

DANNY: You're alive.

GERARD: But I'm not the same Dan. I wont ever be the same, will I? This fucking fucker won't fucking well fuck! I've just got to get over it.

DANNY: Is that what the Doctor's saying?

GERARD: No. My mates. I'm going to get stamped as unfit. Danny, if my memory goes does that mean I no longer exist?

DANNY: That's a hard one.

GERARD: I don't know what I'm missing until I stumble across it. Bad enough dealing with that without all the rest. Got to tell myself 'Relax, it's just the fucking door'… I need you to move back in with Mum.

DANNY: Wouldn't work.

GERARD: Make it work.

DANNY: Look. Trust me.

GERARD: Why?

DANNY: I can't.

GERARD: Well what then fucken? What am I going to do? Roz can't be here all the time.

DANNY: I make her feel worse.

GERARD: Bullshit, she's your mum.

DANNY: You don't get the face I get.

GERARD: What face? When?

DANNY: I can still see it.

GERARD: Then you've gotta try and…

DANNY: What do you think I'm fucking doing!

GERARD: I get angry with her Dan! Really angry. Over little things. Really angry… it scares her. It scares me. It's hard to keep a lid on. I'm not myself. She reckons when she's walked into my room for something and I've woken up, I've followed her around the room, watching her, watching what she did, and she says, it's not like having her son watch her, y'know… It's like someone else. I was outside a couple of nights ago. Couldn't sleep or… anyway something's made me look down the side of the house and I've seen something. I thought 'What the fuck's that?' Looks like a floating head.

DANNY: A ghost?

GERARD: Then it's clicked. It's some fucking… guy peering in at Mum through the blinds.

DANNY: Who is? What guy?

GERARD: I've started walking towards him. 'What the fuck are you doing?' And he bolts. I take off after him down the side of the house bouncing off the wall and the bloody fence and when I've hit the footpath I've tried to go round the corner and I couldn't. I tried but I couldn't. Couldn't turn left. I've run straight into the fucking… wheelie bin out front. And he's gone. Bolting off like it's the fucking Stawell Gift and I'm down on all fours covered in shit. All I could do was yell after him 'I've spotted you mate!'

DANNY: Did you get a good look at him?

GERARD: No… I called him mate.

DANNY: Jeez, he's lucky mum didn't spot him.

GERARD: She doesn't know.

DANNY: She would have boxed his ears.

GERARD: Oh yeah. She's ready to go up a division to flyweight. When was the last time you saw her?

DANNY: Okay. I'll drop round tonight. I can't promise anything more.

GERARD: Fuck! Danny that'll do!

SCENE EIGHTEEN

DANNY *stands outside the door of his Mum's house. He whispers a poem.*

DANNY: For Dad there was no single magic. My life's not gold or stones you said.

You still had half of it to go when she found you.

Lying on the steps.

From its grief the useless sky, drops of rain were falling on your feet.

Years spun past like fire and shadows
to leave a different air inside me.

I drifted away by standing still.

Pause.

Mum's. We all moved down here a year after Dad died. His sisters were all here. Bit of a shock, big Queenslander to a box with a lid. We were a funny little lot tramping around together, sharing colds, and everything else. Hating each other, which is never for keeps. I had it all going on for a while, old Ducati, in a band. 'The Yard Apes.' Very big in Evans Street. I went a bit off the rails…

well… big derailment, hundreds killed. All happened very quickly. I started panicking over everything. I thought a lot of things would kill me but not fear. Little things. I'd lie low and get on the ink. I never begged or ate out of bins. I didn't mean to end up here but I'm on the rise.

He points to the heavens and whistles. He stops as he notices his watch.

I don't have much left of Dad's. Well this. His watch. It stopped on the day. 10.33 am. Didn't even make it to lunch. He had the facing off a power point. Re-wiring. He was making me watch, as he always did but I'd just float off into my head. I wandered off. Mum found me downstairs standing on a couple of boxes. I turned the mains back on I don't know why… I thought he asked me to do it. I thought I was helping. Mum kept telling me it wasn't my fault, but I killed him. I killed her husband. He was so good at everything. Imagine killing your hero… I couldn't stop writing his name everywhere, on everything. I was like a vandal. When we went to the funeral home, Mum had to be helped. It was like an acre of caskets, some open some closed. Gerard thought Dad was inside one of them, but of course he wasn't. We all had dreams about him coming back. Especially Roz. That it had been mistaken identity at the hospital. Some other guy. All back to normal. Gerard wasn't told all the facts. He was just a little kid. He was the youngest, so it was decided and that was that. Can't blame Mum, she was in shock. She just wanted to give us all a chance to stay together. She would go to her grave before she told… which is why when I could I left. I couldn't look at her anymore.

I kept a track of it and so far she has lived twenty-eight years without the man she loved. The only other thing I got is Granddad's campaign medal from Belgium, 1916. I kept it, shouldn't have but I thought it would keep me safe or bring me luck… something. I guess it has. Living on the streets is a death-defying act. Gerard should have it. I've got to tell him. A bit of show and tell with someone trained to kill. Oh brother.

SCENE NINETEEN

The CORPORAL *is seated on the bench, he seems listless.*

MAJOR: Corporal, at ease. Major Sneaky manoeuvre. Good news. Today a manoeuvre crack-brained enough to win you the iron cross and thrill you skinny in the process. So unsettling in it's turpitude that on having it explained, grown men have been known to simply wander off into the night.

CORPORAL: When do we start Sir?

MAJOR: The tonsillectomy has been performed by almost anyone with opposable thumbs. It has never I believe been executed in tandem with a Brazilian wax on the Western lowlands gorilla.

CORPORAL: Tricky customer Sir.

MAJOR: Using only cloves as an anaesthetic you will need to prep the alpha male of the group. This can only be achieved if you mimic perfectly the behaviour of the dominant female and lure him into a prone position.

CORPORAL: And the hard part Sir?

MAJOR: Now the hard part. Torture any man and he will eventually tell you that being waxed is his second greatest fear. Well imagine what nightmares invade our hairy friends sleep.

CORPORAL: I can't Sir.

MAJOR: Once you've established a rapport with the Silverback, the most unpredictable of the Congo primates, you must signal by using eye contact or the code phrase 'I feel like there are ten hands on me'. If the layman has any doubts, now is the time to retreat or work out the most comfortable position for your imminent death. But if you were Major Sneaky Manoeuvre the wax would be hot, the mattock honed to a keen edge and you'd be hurtling towards the patient on a log slide.

CORPORAL: Understood Sir.

MAJOR: The operation takes a mere second with the tools we're using as long as the jaws of the male remain relaxed. It's the waxing that requires patience and a firm hand, and once you've started you don't stop. In three hastily rent tugs the job is done.

Any idea of your escape at this stage would only be entertained by the deranged or infirm, but if you're lucky enough to get one more lungful of air, my guess is you should try to reason your way out with successive uppercuts followed by a jinking weaving—

GERARD *rises and leaves.*

... Sprint towards the nearest body of water, and Corporal? Let's not end up with a wet arse and no fish. Dismissed.

SCENE TWENTY

The park. GERARD *sits on the bench. He reads a paper.* DANNY *enters.*

DANNY: Gerard.

GERARD: Where you been?

DANNY: Zoo.

GERARD: Catch up with the rellies?

DANNY: Yeah.

GERARD: They let you sell there?

DANNY: I don't sell. I wouldn't sell there. Couldn't make it last night.

GERARD: Lucky I didn't tell Mum you were coming. I actually thought you'd show. Lost twenty bucks to Roz. You owe me.

DANNY: I had to help a friend out. He was in a bit of strife.

GERARD: Like I said, you owe me.

DANNY: Gerard I've got to tell you something—

GERARD: Are you coming down to the march? Mum can't and Roz is going to stay with her.

DANNY: I got to work my pitch.

GERARD: It's a public holiday.

DANNY: For the public. It's a good selling day. I can make sixty dollars. Then I can take you down to The Meikong and get a special fried rice and a good whack of sweet and sour and we'll mix the two like before. Lots of pork, pineapple, we love pineapple, remember? It's the only fruit we would eat hot.

GERARD: No wonder you've stacked it on.

DANNY: I like a bit of fat, it keeps me warm at night.

GERARD: That's all that keeps you warm at night.

DANNY: Happy that way.

GERARD: Happy alone?

DANNY: I'm not alone.

GERARD: Happy talking to yourself?

DANNY: Aren't you? Get more sense. I talk to lots of people.

GERARD: But do they answer back?

DANNY: You can get fucked. I just wanted to shout you dinner. Now you're out of the army you're a smart arse.

GERARD: I'm still in the fucking army. Don't talk to me about the army.

DANNY: You bring it up.

GERARD: You wouldn't have made it in the army.

DANNY: Wouldn't want to.

GERARD: You haven't got the guts.

DANNY: Plenty of guts.

GERARD: That's fucken sweet and sour pork's done that.

DANNY: I got guts.

GERARD: You tear up over a dead bird on the road.

DANNY: They're squashed but the wind still made their wings flap.

GERARD: Fuck really! I saw guys pulling shrapnel out of themselves!

DANNY: No kidding!

GERARD: I saw fire fuse people's heads together.

DANNY: Woo hoo!

GERARD: I saw skinless people.

DANNY: Yeah? Who were they?!

GERARD: How the fuck should I know?

DANNY: Gerard—

GERARD: Don't start.

DANNY: You're going to kill me but I'm going to tell you about Dad.

GERARD: Dad? I've been having dreams about him. I had the same one about three nights in a row then never again. This one… This weird one. I'm driving through the main street of Khost in a flat bed. I'm carrying this load of apples and ammo.

DANNY: Dangerous.

GERARD: So I have to drive carefully cause everything's rolling around back there and all the local kids are running after me and shouting and yelling and I'm telling them not to take any in case they picked up a live round and all of a sudden Dad steps out of this house. This mud-brick place. And tells everyone to shut up because he can't hear the trots on his trannie. And I start slowing down cos I'm thinking where the fuck did you come from and there's this whump and the sky goes red. Then black like your telly going off. And when it comes back on I'm lying there on the street yelling 'Ambush left! Ambush left!' There's explosions going off and smoke everywhere and there's this spray shooting up in the air and I think there goes the hydraulic line on the truck we're stuck here but it's really the artery on my leg. I hear one of the guys running up yelling my name and all he can say is 'Holy fuck!' I'm thinking don't say Holy Fuck mate, that's not good. I'm starting to think this is it. I'm going to die here in the dirt, and all around me there's no kids anymore. No kids. Just their shoes. I look over at Kenny, and there was blood all over his face and I said, 'My leg's gone. My leg's out on the road back there' and he says 'Least of your worries mate, your Dad's fucking ropeable'. There's blood just pumping out of me and it's mixing in with all the fuel and I'm trying to keep it separated and Dad's there and he's gets fair in to me for losing all this blood and he says 'You're fucked. I wouldn't go buying any green bananas'. I laugh. Every night I laughed like he used to make me, but when I look at him closely he's holding the body of this little boy. He's got blue eyes and a yellow shirt. He likes apples, he says, only fruit. He would only eat fruit. And Dad says 'What can you do about it?' And I can feel me dying. I can feel everything sinking out of me and it's terrifying. I can't do anything about it so I stop looking for my leg. That's when I wake up. When I give up looking for my leg I wake up. Three nights in a row then never again…

   Silence.

There was a little Afghan kid. Maybe eight or nine. We called him Noosa cause he was always hanging around. His father was dead. Killed in the war. We'd give him US bucks to help his mum. I told him he should start selling kebabs over the road and we'd all buy them. He set up a stall. He would've been raking it in. Because he was selling to Aussies, that's where they hid the bomb. In his stall.

DANNY: Oh.

GERARD: You don't expect to see kids smashed to pieces. What am I going to do? Danny I'm… scared I don't want to go back.

DANNY: You got the march tomorrow. I reckon it'll all be clearer then.

SCENE TWENTY-ONE

GERARD *is sitting on the footpath outside his mother's house. He holds a bottle and rolls it around on its base.*

GERARD: Left… right… left, right, left…

> DANNY *enters. He wears a secondhand suit and his hair is combed. His grandfather's medal is pinned to his chest.*

DANNY: Gerard… Mate. What are you still doing here? Your lift? Who was it? You were telling me. The Unknown Soldier. Which was rude of me. You pulled me up on that one. And I got to tell you, Gerard I wouldn't have made a good soldier I know. I mean I've killed stuff, what little boy… hasn't?

GERARD: They forgot me.

DANNY: Huh?

GERARD: I've disappeared.

DANNY: You're not going to the march?

GERARD: They forgot to pick me up.

DANNY: Is Mum inside? I'll get you there. I'll get a cab. We can… is that Galliano?

GERARD: It's Roz's.

DANNY: Should you be drinking that?

GERARD: Not with the pills I'm on. [*He takes a deep slug.*] Anyway, I'm not going. Should have seen this coming eh? Dad left me. You left me. Now the force. Got the fucking trifecta.

DANNY: You're not drinking that shit. C'mon, we can do something inside. We're family.

GERARD: Inside?

DANNY: I've come over to see Mum. Yeah… I was going to drop a little something off to her. She'll get a shock… It's… it's Dad's watch. C'mon, we'll have a tea and watch it on tele.

GERARD: You want to go inside?

DANNY: Hey tomorrow we could go to the zoo. All of us. Mum, you, me and Roz. Together. I'll show you all the monkeys, they're a lot like us y'know and we're a lot like them. One of them even looks like Uncle Greg.

> GERARD *manages a laugh.*

GERARD: Fuck.

DANNY: Here. Who said I couldn't write.

He brings out a magazine.

They finally put me in the mag.
　Stumbled slipped sank like the sun
　Under heavy hung clouds that swell and saddle this darkening
　　day
　Can't stand the night with its absence of you,
　The sky is in misery the stars are a mess.

GERARD: Who's that about?

GERARD *stands up and puts his hand on* DANNY*'s shoulder. They share a smile.* GERARD *turns and begins to walk away from the house.*

DANNY: Hey Gerard... Mum's is this way.

GERARD *turns. They both walk up to the door.* GERARD *signals* DANNY *to go ahead of him.* DANNY *takes a deep breath and enters.*

THE END

Skip Miller's Hit Songs

Sean Riley

Above: Assina Ntawumenya as Patience Lugor in the 2011 Brink production at Odeon Theatre in Adelaide. Below: Mondli Makhoba as Augustus Forkay in the 2011 Brink production at Odeon Theatre in Adelaide.
(Photos: Chris Herzfeld)

Introduction

The seed for *Skip Miller's Hit Songs* was laid during the early hours of the morning whilst channel surfing television. I stumbled across a documentary that chronicled an Australian journalist's experiences in Rwanda at the height of the civil war that ravaged the country in the early nineteen nineties. Grim, yes; and whilst others would keep surfing in the hope of stumbling across lighter fare, such material is gripping and strangely nourishing to me (see below for further explanation).

Towards the end of the documentary, the journalist and his crew drive into a deserted village, post massacre. Alighting from their vehicle, the journalist walks away from the cameraman's lens, down the main street, through the carnage, his eyes calmly scanning the ground for any signs of life, but finding none. He turns back to the camera and shrugs, shaking his head. I'm thinking '*How immune to the horrors of war is this man? What about your heart? What happens to your heart? Is it made of granite?*'

But then, suddenly, from behind a building, a small child, a girl, four years old at the most, scurries out onto the street, makes a b-line for the journalist and takes his hand. What ensues is one of the most powerful moments of journalism I've ever witnessed. As the camera draws nearer, the journalist totally unravels, his heart suddenly giving way, unable to speak, his body wracked by sobs. The child watches him in silence, her tiny hand still gripping his as he attempts to speak to the cameraman; his words an unintelligible groan. It's an appalling vision: disturbing, voyeuristic, and I'm completely gripped and on the edge of my seat. The seed was sewn.

Inspiration for a new work rarely hits me like a thunderbolt. It's a much slower, scatter-gun process; images, random statements, obscure news stories, or even particular passages of music collect and remain, clinging, like barnacles, around those aspects of human existence I find unfathomable. It's all about what gets under my skin; what itches and festers away, that causes me to sit down and write it out, by way of attempting to make sense of the madness.

It's important, as a writer, to know *why* you write; the concerns you're wrestling with, the themes you keep returning to, the axe you have to grind, the mystery you're seeking to understand. The reasons are experiential, usually stemming from childhood, and have their beginnings in those cataclysmic moments where the normality and certainty of life cracks open like an abyss before you.

My abyss opened in 1975, when I was eight years old, and living on the North West Coast of Tasmania. My parents went on a trip to Port Arthur, the historic ruins of the draconian penal colony the bottom of the island. As a gift, they brought me home a ghoulish souvenir; a blood-red brick, from the children's infirmary, bearing a ghostly thumb-print the exact same size as mine. 'Isn't it amazing?', my parents cooed in innocent wonder. 'It fits you like a glove.' I'd like to say I smiled and accepted the gift with grace, but instead I began sobbing hysterically—an outburst which lasted for several hours. My eyes were suddenly opened to how appallingly people treat each other, and from that moment on, I became a 'misery sponge': books, documentaries and movies (all united by their grim subjects) were devoured, not for titillation, I must stress, but in the endless search for understanding of the source of human cruelty, and, ultimately, human resilience… Hence the journalist unravelling on the abandoned street in Rwanda. All of my works wrestle with this notion; people don't like other people. But I'm always searching for the contradiction, the opposite.

I always draw my inspiration visually, with a particular focus on photojournalism. If you want a visual introduction to *Skip Miller's Hit Songs*, please seek out images from the following: Robert Capa, Inge Morath, Sebastiao Salgado, Tim Hetherington, Gordon Parks, Ashley Gilbertson, Larry Burrows, Josef Koudelka, Susan Meiselas… just to name a few.

Photojournalism—good photojournalism—is an act of protest. Writing—good writing—is a form of protest also. But the creation of our works could not be more different. One is passive and introspective, the other relentless and life-threatening. I have an undying admiration for photojournalists. They chase danger, infiltrate the volcanic epicentres of some of the most horrendous and shameful moments in world history, chasing that one iconic image that will define years of conflict and human suffering. And then, when the assignment ends, they come home. Back to normality. Or do they? Are they forever caught between two worlds?

When Brink Productions' Artistic Director Chris Drummond asked me to pitch a work to him in 2009 my response was swift, and my vision shared by Chris and his company. I wanted to write an ensemble piece that explored, through dialogue, imagery and music, the psyche of a frontline photojournalist, as well as the lives of those he has touched—be it as subjects of his work, his lover, family and associates.

The choice of Africa as Skip's stomping ground was motivated by the growing influx of refugees from varying African nations into Adelaide at the time. I continue to be delighted by the growing community of African immigrants in South Australia. I love the diversity, the colour, and the wealth of experience they bring to our city. I wanted more than anything, through this work, to see that vibrancy reflected on a stage, to tell their stories, and explore the personal minutia of African–Australian relationships in a theatrical context, laced with two qualities I never leave home without—heart and humour.

In the central character of Skip Miller, I found an endlessly rich (and challenging) character through which to explore these ideas and themes. A hardened and obsessive photojournalist, returning home, and falling apart, unable to resolve the past, unable to move forward. Similarly, the characters in Skip's immediate circle are, in their own ways, caught between two worlds, be they actual or metaphorical. Scratch below the surface of the play, and you find it is all about the endless search for identity. The best theatre holds a mirror up to the audience, and communicates that one undeniable truth; we are all the same, no matter what our race, gender, or experience.

As the great photojournalist Robert Capa said, 'If your photographs aren't good enough, you're not close enough'. This axiom was reflected in the process of bringing *Skip Miller's Hit Songs* to the stage. It was a rigorous, lengthy, arduous, terrifying, frustrating, life-changing experience. I am forever indebted to my collaborators, most particularly Chris Drummond and the amazing cast—all unrelenting in the quest for truth.

Sean Riley
2012.

For Kim

Skip Miller's Hit Songs was commissioned and first produced by Brink Productions at the Odeon Theatre, Norwood, South Australia, on 16 February 2011, with the following cast, in order of appearance.

SKIP MILLER	Chris Pitman
PATIENCE LUGOR	Assina Ntawumenya
NEVILLE MILLER	Rory Walker
AUGUSTUS FORKAY	Mondli Makhoba
ALISON CALDICOTT	Lizzy Falkland
BASEL MGEMBE	Adolphus Waylee
MUSICIANS	Quentin Grant
	Jerome Lyons
	Lamine Nanky

Director/Dramaturg, Chris Drummond
Designer, Wendy Todd
Music Director, Quentin Grant
Filmmaker, James Kalisch
Lighting Designer, Geoff Cobham
Producer, Kay Jamieson

CHARACTERS

SKIP MILLER, early 40s

ALISON CALDICOTT, late 30s

BASEL MGEMBE, early 20s

NEVILLE MILLER, mid 40s

PATIENCE LUGOR, mid 30s

AUGUSTUS FORKAY, early 40s

MUSICIANS

SETTING

The action moves between various locations in Africa and Australia. The set should be suggestive and makeshift, and, in keeping with the photojournalism themes, the premiere production made extensive use of film projections. These projections are detailed in the stage directions.

Prologue. Africa 2010. A marketplace. Food, chatter, bartering, music, dancing. The actors and musicians interact with the audience. A funeral passes by.

Music. SKIP *stands central, his face illuminated. Moving images of African faces, illuminated by candles, move slowly above him. They are captured on sheets of paper, and trajectories are followed under the following.*

SKIP: There are times when you're suddenly invisible
    Heart pounding in your ears
    You disappear.
    In a heady rush
    You're able to just… observe.
    Witness
    Surrounded by the worst that humankind can serve up…
    The pack is one and you're not part of it
    You're free to get on and do your job.
    They submit.
    Turn their gaze.
    Their shame horror rage terror towards the lens.
    Not me; the lens.
    It's as if they want you to record—
    Both sides—
    'Look at me', they say.
    'Record me.'
    'The last of me'
    'Before I'm taken'
    'Before I'm hacked to pieces by the mob.'
    'Before I turn my back and walk away…'
At that moment it's my duty, as a human being, to do what I do.

    PATIENCE *is there.* SKIP *is gone. The entire back wall is a tight close up of* PATIENCE*'s face—a detail of the shot* SKIP *took of her, years before. It grows in slow motion around her.*

PATIENCE: It is a strange thing to arrive in a new country and find that everyone knows your face. I am the girl. In the picture. A moment. A brief moment in time, captured in the click of his camera. I am everywhere. In the newspapers. In the magazines. On bus shelters. On the wall of the gallery. Just when I think that girl is gone, here she is again—everywhere I look. I thought the distance would erase her. I do all they ask of me. I shake hands. I smile for the cameras. I answer their questions. It is like a loud dream. A strange and difficult welcome.

Australia. Skip Miller Photographic Exhibition. Through a projected doorway we see people milling about. PATIENCE *stands outside, closer to the audience.* SKIP *approaches* PATIENCE *as the door dissolves into nothingness.*

SKIP: You okay?

PATIENCE: [*nodding*] Oh, yes. You?

SKIP: [*shaking his head*] I want to run away and hide. Would you like a drink?

PATIENCE: Your brother is getting one for me.

SKIP: Is he? Right. Good. That's good. [*Pause.*] Thank you. For coming.

PATIENCE: Thank you. For inviting me. And making sure I got here.

SKIP: Thank my agent for that. And everyone else. In between. Here and there. Pulling strings.

>   *Silence.*

PATIENCE: They are lovely photographs.

SKIP: Ya reckon?

>   *Silence.*

PATIENCE: I'm sorry that I do not remember you.

SKIP: [*shrugging*] I'm a pretty forgettable kinda guy.

>   PATIENCE *laughs.* NEVILLE *enters, with two drinks.*

But here's a kinda guy who's *un*forgettable!

NEVILLE: Champagne.

PATIENCE: Thank you.

NEVILLE: Cheers.

NEVILLE *chinks his glass against hers and drinks.*

PATIENCE: I beg your pardon?

NEVILLE: It's a custom. You—

NEVILLE *chinks her glass again and drinks—to demonstrate.*
SKIP *raises his glass.*

SKIP: Cheers.

PATIENCE: Okay.

PATIENCE *drinks warily.*

NEVILLE: I've got my tickets for the footy tomorrow night.

SKIP: Oh yeah?

NEVILLE: [*to* SKIP] Mm. [*To* PATIENCE] Australian Rules Football.
Magnificent game... I've got a spare ticket. If you want.

PATIENCE *nods.*

PATIENCE: Can we walk?

NEVILLE: [*a beat behind*] Okay. Sure. Or I could pick you up.

Beat.

In my car.

PATIENCE: No. I mean around here. The exhibition. Walk. Around.

NEVILLE: Ah! [*Laughing*] Right... May I?

PATIENCE: Okay.

AUGUSTUS *enters as* SKIP *watches* PATIENCE *and* NEVILLE *go.*

AUGUSTUS: Where are you?

SKIP: Huh?

AUGUSTUS: You look like you want to be somewhere else.

SKIP: So do you.

Pause.

I want to be at home. In my beach shack. Wind whistling under
the door. Kettle boiling on the range. The waves crashing like soft
thunder on the shore. The delicate crunch of sand under foot.

AUGUSTUS: Skippy—this is a love poem.

SKIP: Free of sound and fury. In my dark room.

AUGUSTUS: Crazy old dinosaur.

SKIP: I enjoy it. The magic of it. Alchemy.

AUGUSTUS: Uh huh.

SKIP: Some I shoot for myself. How's your world?

AUGUSTUS: [*sarcastic*] Mind blowing! Ringworm cream and methadone.

SKIP: Shit. Frontline action at the pharmacy.

AUGUSTUS: Nowhere to hide.

SKIP: Might have to come around and shoot it.

AUGUSTUS: I smell another Walkley!

SKIP: O great sun oracle.

> ALISON *enters and walks right up to* SKIP.

Hi.

> ALISON *kisses him, deeply. Then pulls back.*

Sorry. Have we met?

> AUGUSTUS *laughs.*

ALISON: Alison. Caldicott.

SKIP: Skip. Miller.

ALISON: You wanna go round wiv me?

SKIP: I bet you were a total slapper at high school.

ALISON: Well, I'm not a masochistic doormat. Or a desperate man-chasing nympho.

SKIP: That's not what I've heard.

ALISON: So what'd'ya reckon? You wanna go round wiv me?

SKIP: Okay. But I'll leave. I'll always leave.

> BASEL *runs into the space wearing a dress. He slams against the wall, frozen in terror.*

ALISON: You'll have to come back first though, won't you?

SKIP: Jeez, this champagne's shit, isn't it?

Music of a town besieged. Projection: the point of view a boy racing through high grass is projected onto BASEL's *chest.* AUGUSTUS *turns to the audience.*

AUGUSTUS: On the outskirts of Bandele, a town in northwestern Liberia. The air is hot and still. The shadows grow long. A woman stands facing a boy—dust glistens between them in the air.

BASEL: Mama said, *'Put it on'.*

I think, 'Has she gone crazy?'

I'm just a boy.

My sisters have gone to fetch water.

'Put it on', she says.

She is fast and rough.

I'm a doll in her hands.

'Is this a game?'

'You'll be safer', she says. *'It's men they're after. Put it on. Or they'll take you.'*

I ask, *'Who? Who will take me?'*

I do not know the rules of this game.

MAMA says, *'There! You look like a girl!'*

'I look like a boy. In a dress.'

'No. You look like an ugly girl.'

'As ugly as cousin Poni?'

'Not quite. But close', she says.

'What do we do now? What do we do next?'

She says nothing. She takes my hand and leads me through the back door.

Outside.

We run. As fast as we can. Through high grass.

And now I know this is not a game.

BASEL *is gone. Return to Skip Miller Photographic Exhibition.*

AUGUSTUS: Drink?

SKIP: Sure. Whatever.

AUGUSTUS: Crack pipe?

SKIP: Yo, Bro! Pack it, let's stack it!

AUGUSTUS: [*exiting*] Man, you're shit at being cool.

AUGUSTUS *walks away.*

SKIP: At least I've got hair!

>*Silence.*

When is it?

ALISON: Next Thursday.

SKIP: Thursday. Looming. Imminent.

ALISON: You make it sound like a lumber-puncture.

SKIP: Don't you think it's a bit weird being interviewed by my own girlfriend?

ALISON: That's what they want.

SKIP: What sort of questions are you going to ask me?

ALISON: All sorts of sordid shit.

SKIP: Like what?

ALISON: You tell me. I'm a front end loader for dirty laundry.

SKIP: So I've heard.

>ALISON *points to a photograph adorning a wall.*

ALISON: I like that one.

SKIP: Yeah?

ALISON: Yes. It's nice.

SKIP: [*flatly*] Nice.

ALISON: Compared to the others, yes. He's smiling. He's saying 'I am indestructible'… Call me old-fashioned, but dead bodies make me squeamish.

SKIP: Wuss.

>BASEL *enters and squats.*

ALISON: Can I have it?

SKIP: Depends.

ALISON: On what?

>SKIP *laughs and wanders off as* NEVILLE *enters past, champagne glasses in his hand.*

[*To* NEVILLE] Your brother is such a shit.

NEVILLE: Tell me something I don't know.

ALISON: [*to* SKIP] On what?

>SKIP *laughs as he is followed off by* ALISON.

NEVILLE: Night. Bandele, Northwestern Liberia. The roar of fire and gunshot, the air thick with smoke.

BASEL *crouches at the bottom of a ditch, eyes heavenward.*

BASEL: The ditch smells of blood and sweat. The heavy footfall of men, all around us. The pounding of my Mama's heart. *'Play dead!'* she hissed. *'Do not move a muscle!'* I close my eyes and see the faces of my sisters and pray that they are alive, playing dead, lying face down in ditches, waiting for light. For the smoke to clear. For the danger to pass. Or are they beneath us already? On whom do we rest? One by one, the faces of my friends, their families, our village, flicker against my eyelids. Beneath me, I feel the bodies move. A small shift of limbs, a struggle, beneath my arm. I feel breath against my finger tips. I stretch my fingers, slowly. And touch the lips that breathe, gently, a silent message. The breath grows faster, catches—in what? Laughter? Relief? Fear? I keep my fingers against the lips. Feel the warm breath, a rhythm, a comfort, like a clock, as the night passes by. In the early hours, before sunrise, it stops. No choke, no sigh. Just a small gasp that is never released.

Music. Neville's shop, Halcyon Daze. Australia. SKIP *rummages through a large basket of tiny china dolls.* NEVILLE *holds up a tin aeroplane, circa 1950s.*

NEVILLE: What do you think? For Will. He's aeroplane mad. At the moment.
SKIP: Is he?
NEVILLE: Too far away.

Silence.

SKIP: Where did these come from?
NEVILLE: You remember Vessinger's Bakery?
SKIP: Yeah—vanilla slice—
NEVILLE: Caw! Jaffa cakes—

SKIP: Baw! Matchsticks—

NEVILLE: Maw! Natalie Vessinger's rack—

SKIP & NEVILLE: [*together*] Faw!

>   *They laugh.*

NEVILLE: She walked past last week.

SKIP: Who? Natalie Vessinger?

NEVILLE: Mmm. Alas! Time has not been kind to Natalie. Or her rack.

>   SKIP *grunts the shame of it.*

Anyway, it's being ripped down to make way for apartments.

SKIP: Her rack?

NEVILLE: The Bakery. Soon to be luxury penthouse accommodation. Greedy, history killing, capitalist bastards. They ripped up the floorboards, only to discover hundreds of these [*Indicating the dolls*] underneath. The building was a doll factory in the late eighteen hundreds. I couldn't resist. I have boxes of them... They've been sleeping. Under a layer of flour and sugar. All this time. Over a century. Waiting. For sunlight to touch their porcelain cheeks.

>   SKIP *moves onto a box of old photographs.* NEVILLE *adjusts the basket of dolls.*

SKIP: You wanna come for lunch on Sunday?

NEVILLE: No can do Sunday.

SKIP: Got a Toy Train Convention to go to, have you?

NEVILLE: No. [*He coughs.*] I've got a date.

>   *Pause.*

SKIP: [*smirking*] Ooh. Ooooh.

NEVILLE: Shuddup.

SKIP: [*suddenly twelve*] Oooo-ooh! Lov-ers!

NEVILLE: Don't make a big deal about it.

SKIP: Who is she?

NEVILLE: Early stages. Don't want to ruin it.

SKIP: How can telling your brother ruin it?

NEVILLE: Because I don't know what it is. Yet. What I'm doing. If I can. Do it.

SKIP: It?

NEVILLE: Courting. Romance. Act One.

SKIP: You need some advice?

NEVILLE: From *you*? [*He laughs derisively.*] No thanks.

SKIP: What's her name?

NEVILLE: I don't know if she's even interested—

SKIP: What's her name?

NEVILLE: Patience. It's Patience.

    Pause.

SKIP: Jesus—

NEVILLE: Like I said—

SKIP: Wow.

NEVILLE: Early days—

SKIP: Perfect. That's perfect... It's fantastic.

NEVILLE: We'll see... Don't—I just—

SKIP: Yeah, yeah. Okay... Patience. Wow.

    Silence.

NEVILLE: What happened?

SKIP: Happened?

NEVILLE: The day you met her. Took the picture. What happened to her?

SKIP: I'm not going to tell you that. It's not my story to tell.

NEVILLE: I just want to know. Fill in the details.

SKIP: Yep.

NEVILLE: Right. You took—

SKIP: I just took the picture.

NEVILLE: Right.

    Pause.

  Did you speak to her?

SKIP: No.

NEVILLE: Right. Did she say anything?

SKIP: No.

NEVILLE: Right.

SKIP: There were aid workers. Of which I am not one.

    BASEL *enters.*

NEVILLE: Of course. I know that. I know that. I know what you do. [*Pause.*] And what you don't do.

SKIP: Drop it, Fido.

Projection: an endless parade of human shadows begin passing across BASEL.

NEVILLE: I'm not very good at it, I don't think. Relationships. I scare people off. I never say the right thing. I laugh at the wrong time. I pack the wrong sorts of sandwiches. I ask too many questions. Only because I want to know. I'm interested. Fascinated. I like talking. To people. I can't help it.

SKIP: I know.

NEVILLE: Never bloody shut up. That's why Miranda left me. Cause I talked too much.

SKIP: No, Miranda left you because she was a deceitful, cheating bitch.

NEVILLE: Yeah. Alright. Point taken.

They laugh.

SKIP: Cut yourself some slack, mate. Don't rush things. Have patience.

They laugh.

Music. Projections of an endless river of people continue to pass across BASEL.

BASEL: We walk for days, my Mama and I, in a river of people to the camp. Sleep is scarce, short bursts, in ditches, beneath trees. Hidden from those who follow. A silent journey. We do not speak of what is behind. We do not speak of what is ahead. Our breath saved only for walking. At the gates of the camp, between high wire fences, Mama stops, and lets go of my hand.

The projections cease.

'Not much further, Mama. Then you can sleep.' But she takes my face in her hands, a grip, her forehead against mine. *'I have to go back to find my girls.'* Her eyes full of tears. And so I say nothing. She tells me I will be safe. She tells me that I am a man now. She tells me to be good. And stay out of trouble. She tells me—

BASEL *runs forward; suddenly a young boy, with eyes full of tears and fear.*

[*In Kreyol*] Mama! Take me with you, Mama! Please! Do not leave me! I am not a man! I am a boy! Mama!

Silence as he watches his mother disappear from view.

Australia. A television studio. Pre-interview. A large projected portrait of SKIP, *camera poised.* SKIP *and* ALISON *seated opposite each other.*

ALISON: [*his portrait*] You like it?

SKIP: Bit much, isn't it?

ALISON: What? Not your favourite?

SKIP: Bloody poser.

ALISON: No. It's you.

SKIP: No. It isn't.

ALISON: I like it. Bit of hot journo crumpet. Sweat and dust. War-torn Walkley Award-Winning Hot Spot Poster Boy. The viewers'll love it.

A TECHNICIAN *adjusts* SKIP*'s microphone pinned to his collar.*

You nervous?

SKIP: No.

ALISON: Good.

SKIP: Should I be?

ALISON *cackles like a witch.* SKIP *laughs.*

ALISON: You want water?

SKIP: No.

ALISON: You'll need water.

SKIP: Will I?

ALISON: [*an order*] He needs water.

A PRODUCTION ASSISTANT *exits in search of water.*

ALISON: Try not to bump your mic, by the way. Had Bob Ellis on last week. He rustled like a bloody tree.

SKIP *laughs.*

Nice tie.

SKIP: Ya reckon?

ALISON: Yeah. What exquisitely tasteful individual bought that for you?
SKIP: Dunno. Can't remember her name.

> ALISON *laughs.*

TECHNICIAN: Going in four—
SKIP: Be nice.
TECHNICIAN: Three.
ALISON: Sure.
TECHNICIAN: Two.
SKIP: Give us a kiss.
ALISON: Shuddup.
TECHNICIAN: One.

NEVILLE, *with a football scarf and blanket. He's waiting. The image of Will, his son, aged 6, near him. He wears a beanie and scarf also.* NEVILLE *watches as he walks off in the other direction. A dog barks from the distance.* PATIENCE *enters, opposite. They sit on chairs. Suddenly a crowded stadium. Clouds against a blue winter sky are projected.*

NEVILLE: Nice view.
PATIENCE: Yes. Beautiful.
NEVILLE: Quite a climb.
PATIENCE: Yes.
NEVILLE: Sorry about that. Every year I ask for better tickets, but—
PATIENCE: Oh, it's no problem. I wanted to come.
NEVILLE: Hungry?

> PATIENCE *nodding.* NEVILLE *offers his lunchbox.*

Chicken, mayo and rocket.
PATIENCE: Uh huh.

> *They eat.*

Next time it's my turn.

> PATIENCE *looks over the edge.*

You come to the footy often?

NEVILLE: Yeah. Reduces stress levels.

PATIENCE *laughs.*

PATIENCE: I think many people here are sad and afraid. I cannot believe how no-one smiles.

NEVILLE: Really?

PATIENCE: Back home everybody smiled.

NEVILLE: I smiled at a little old lady last week outside the shop. She covered her handbag underneath her cardigan and crossed the street.

The siren sounds.

Here we go!

The crowd roars.

[*Standing*] C'mon!

Music. The crowd fades into the distance.

PATIENCE: Ringari, a small pineapple-growing village in Muyinga Province, Burundi. Nine thirty a.m. A classroom.

It is the start of the day. The best hours. The coolest. When minds are alert.

Twenty-six children are seated before me, awaiting inspiration.

Fifty-two glistening eyes awaiting my next move.

I know everyone of them, inside out.

This morning's lesson is one for fun.

She holds a sheet of paper aloft.

Paper aeroplane making!

She begins folding the paper.

Each child follows my instructions.

They are keen. Inspired. And quiet. So quiet…

Except for Desiree Kwizera, who never shuts up—

I say to her—*'Girl, you want to move your tongue, fold paper with it!'*

She folds.

At times like these I know I am a good teacher.

In the silence. Only the sound of children's hands at work

And a dog barking on the road outside.

She completes her work, stands, and launches it, the air above them filled with paper planes.

Twenty-six paper planes are launched, and the whitewashed room becomes the sky.

The crowd roars, and NEVILLE *leaps to his feet beside her.*

NEVILLE: Yes!!

She looks at him.

Gripping, isn't it?

PATIENCE: Oh, yes.

NEVILLE: I knew you'd enjoy it. You want a pie?

The crowd roars.

Australia. Post interview. SKIP *and* ALISON. SKIP *is furious.*

SKIP: What the fuck was that all about?!

ALISON: I'm sorry if you expected a love-in. I don't do love-ins. You're fair game. You know that. It came up. I asked the question.

SKIP: Fucking *bullshit*?!

ALISON: It was a fair question. It's a grey area. A moral dilemma.

SKIP: Not to me it isn't!

ALISON: Isn't it?

SKIP: What do you mean by that?

ALISON: You continuously say you're invisible. When in actual fact, you're not. You're a white man with a camera. A human being. I just want to know what happens. Without the lens between you and the subject. To the suffering? The misery. What do you do with that? Where do you put it?

SKIP: I leave it, in the ditches at the side of the road with all the dead bodies in Rwanda. And Angola. And Darfur. And Sierra Leone. I bury it. Hide it away. Far away. Another country. That's where I fucking well put it.

ALISON: Do you?

SKIP: Yes I fucking do!

ALISON: Bullshit! You carry it all the way home with you. Excess baggage! You stuff it into boxes and tape them up and hide it all away in every bloody spare spot you can find. One day soon it'll collapse. Cave in. Then you'll be well and truly fucked.

SKIP: I can't believe you did this.

ALISON: What?

SKIP: Did this to me. Turned on me like this.

ALISON: Turned on you? All I did was—

SKIP: Your job! Yes. I know.

ALISON: It shits me; the way you trip off to the far corners to solve the big problems of the world, but you have no idea how to fix your own.

SKIP: *I* have problems?

ALISON: What do you mean by that?

SKIP: I'm not the one hosting a cheesy chat show for middle Australia, am I?

ALISON: You arsehole—

SKIP: B-grade psychoanalysis and water cooler talk may be your idea of success, but it ain't mine, so why don't you crawl out of my arse and crawl up your own and take a peak at your own shit?

> *Pause.*

ALISON: Perhaps you shouldn't have agreed to the interview.

SKIP: No. I shouldn't have.

> SKIP *moves to leave.*

ALISON: Running away to your hut?

SKIP: Fuck you.

> SKIP *exits. Silence.*

ALISON: Fuck you, too.

Australia. Evening. NEVILLE *is saying goodbye to* PATIENCE *after dropping her home after the football.*

NEVILLE: I hope you had a good time.

PATIENCE: Oh, yes. Thank you for taking me.

NEVILLE: My pleasure.

PATIENCE: I am sorry they did not win. Your team.

NEVILLE: They never win. I'm used to it. I live in hope. I'm fiercely loyal.

PATIENCE: Yes. Well—

NEVILLE: Yes! I'll be off then.

PATIENCE: Okay.

> NEVILLE *steps away, awkward, hesitant.*

NEVILLE: I'll call you. Can I call you?

PATIENCE: Yes. Of course. I'd like that.

NEVILLE: Good. Night. I mean, goodnight.

PATIENCE: Goodnight.

> NEVILLE *exits.* PATIENCE *is left alone. She turns and stares into the empty room. The sound of a barking dog from the street outside.*

After the soldiers had finished and gone. After I'd rolled onto my side and picked myself up off the ground. Pulled my torn dress around me. Gathered myself. Back together. After this, I walked. Along the path. Back to the classroom. So silent. And still. I entered. Through the open door. I blinked in the sudden darkness. And I—

All I can smell is blood.

And there they are. In a pile. At the far end of the room. Across the floor. Littered with paper planes. A pile. As if they had tried to climb the wall to escape. I cannot tell one from the other. I cannot tell who is who. I cannot tell—

Halfway up the wall is a pair of hand prints. So small. Stained in blood. Smeared downwards. An attempt at flying…

♦　♦　♦　♦

African sunlight. SKIP *attending to his digital camera, watched by* BASEL.

BASEL: Can I see?

SKIP: Kuankan Refugee Camp, Massanta, Guinea. A city of white tents. Population thirty-three thousand.

BASEL: Can I see?

SKIP: Sure.

He shows him the shots. Silence.

BASEL: It must be nice, doing what you do.

SKIP: Nice?

BASEL: [*the camera*] You are lucky.

Silence as SKIP *checks his pictures taken.*

You go wherever you like.

Pause.

You can go home.

Pause.

SKIP: Yes. I can …

BASEL: You have a lady friend?

Pause.

Why don't you stay home with her?

Pause.

When you are at home, what do you take pictures of?

SKIP: [*off the top of his head*] Swimming pools—

BASEL: [*impressed*] You have a swimming pool?

Pause.

One day I would like a pool. In my own back yard.

SKIP: What's your stroke?

BASEL: Stroke?

SKIP: Freestyle, breaststroke, doggy-paddle?

BASEL: I don't know.

SKIP: Can you actually swim?

BASEL: [*shrugging*] I don't know. I've never tried.

SKIP: Better get that sorted before you get a pool.

BASEL: Will you teach me?

SKIP: What?

BASEL: Teach me.

SKIP: How to swim?

BASEL: No. [*Referring to the camera.*] This. Teach me.

SKIP: Teach you?

BASEL: Take me with you. On the road.

   Pause.

SKIP: How old are you?

BASEL: Twenty-one in two weeks' time.

   SKIP *nodding, considering the possibilities.*

I could be your—what do you call—

SKIP: Interpreter.

BASEL: Interpreter! Win, win. Yes?

   A pause. SKIP *deflates—defeated. He groans, shaking his head, and begins laughing.*

SKIP: Win, win…

Australia. ALISON, *wearing slippers.*

ALISON: Within twenty-four hours of Dad dying, my mother had cleared the house of every sign of him. She whinges about her crippling osteoporosis no end, but somehow managed to get his Jason recliner out onto the back porch by herself. Clothes bagged up. Dressing table cleared and in boxes. I couldn't even smell him… I said, *'I want his slippers.'*

   'What for?'

   'Because they were his. And I want… something of him. Whatever's left.'

   She shoves them at me, and I start to cry. This should be the moment she embraces me, and we stand together, mother and daughter, united in our shared grief for this beautiful man, crying, in silence.

   'Don't!'

   SKIP *enters and begins pegging photos on a makeshift darkroom drying line. The images are of African faces, and they stare out at the audience from the line.*

A hard woman to love, my mother. And then, at the wake, oiled by too much cask moselle, she held court, rhapsodising about their undying love for each other… thirty-eight years of married bliss… Dunno where I was during this time. Certainly don't remember that much love between them. Not from her direction, anyway. The arguments. The compromises. The banality. I promised myself, age sixteen, that I would never do this. Never trap myself, or anyone else, into that life. Joined at the hip. Half of a double act. Always together. With no respite. No distance. Suffocating. Till death do us part. I've chosen this… freedom. Distance.

SKIP*'s beach shack.* AUGUSTUS, NEVILLE *and* SKIP.

SKIP: So what's the prognosis?

AUGUSTUS: Well, to begin with, you look like shit.

SKIP: Thanks.

AUGUSTUS: You're like a mangy old dog.

SKIP: Piss off.

AUGUSTUS: When was the last time you shaved, man?

SKIP: You're just jealous, Baldy!

AUGUSTUS: It's a migraine.

SKIP: Right. [*to* NEVILLE] Told you it was nothing.

NEVILLE: You said you were blind. And numb down your left side.

SKIP: I was. For a bit. Nearly shat myself.

AUGUSTUS: Glad you didn't. Any improvement in your vision?

SKIP: Yes. Patches. Dots. Of colour. Light. Neville looks like a long slice of fairy bread.

    Beat.

Christ! My eyes feel like they're about to shoot out of my head.

NEVILLE: Twelve hours locked in a darkroom may have something to do with that. Plus the intravenous caffeine drip.

AUGUSTUS: How much?

SKIP: I like it! It helps!

AUGUSTUS: How much?

SKIP: [*moaning*] Alright! Too much! Fark! I've got things I need to finish.

AUGUSTUS: You've been drinking water?

SKIP: Yeah.

NEVILLE: With coffee in it—

AUGUSTUS: And your urine?

SKIP: No, just coffee.

AUGUSTUS: How often and what colour?

SKIP: Once a decade. Fluorescent green.

NEVILLE: [*to* AUGUSTUS] It stinks.

SKIP: Jesus—

NEVILLE: It does. Like ammonia.

AUGUSTUS: Life has thrown mud in your eyes. Read the signs. Stop. There's no war here. No deadline. Just cricket and crosswords… if you choose.

SKIP: There are things I need to finish—

AUGUSTUS: Denial is a river in Egypt.

SKIP: Really?

AUGUSTUS: Fall apart a bit, my friend. You need to. Go see a doctor.

SKIP: That's why you're here.

AUGUSTUS: I'm a *pharmacist.*

SKIP: Yeah, yeah. I just want the drugs, not the chat.

AUGUSTUS: Promise me you'll see a doctor.

SKIP: Awright!

AUGUSTUS: You know I'm right. I always am.

SKIP: Yeah, yeah.

AUGUSTUS: In twenty years, have I ever been wrong?

SKIP: Yes.

AUGUSTUS: When?

SKIP: That shirt you bought me for my birthday in ninety-three was pretty hideous.

AUGUSTUS: Yeah. It was.

NEVILLE: I liked it.

SKIP: I'm not going back.

NEVILLE: What?

SKIP: I can't. Anymore. I'm back. For good.

    Pause.

NEVILLE: When did you decide this?

SKIP: The moment the plane lifted off the runway.

Projection of a lone bird, circling in the distant sky.

The moment it all fell away. Beneath me. [*To* AUGUSTUS] The moment I saw you.

AUGUSTUS *clicks like Skippy the Bush Kangaroo.*

AUGUSTUS: Skippy…
SKIP: I'm home. For good.

AUGUSTUS *and* NEVILLE *glance at each other. Silence.*

Africa. SKIP *stares out at the horizon.* BASEL *stands beside him. Silence.*

BASEL: Why are we here?
SKIP: We're waiting.
BASEL: For what?
SKIP: Mr Whippy.
BASEL: Mr Who?
SKIP: Whippy. God On Wheels for all children. He's the Man in the van. That sells ice-cream.
BASEL: Ice-cream?
SKIP: Ice-cream. And chimes.

SKIP *chimes the tune of 'Greensleeves'.*

BASEL: [*speaking over him*] We're waiting for ice-cream?
SKIP: In a perfect world we would be.
BASEL: Here?
SKIP: Especially here. What this country needs is more ice-cream. I dream of Mr Whippy… sometimes… [*Back to the moment*] Got a tip off. Refugees from the north. On the move. Heading our way.

Silence. SKIP *inspects the view through his lens.* BASEL *follows suit.*

The hills… are good.
BASEL: They're just hills.
SKIP: Put a river of people across them though, and they're something else.

SKIP *lowers his camera and adjusts it.*

Sometimes it's not about getting up close. Distance is a powerful thing.

BASEL: Is it?

SKIP: Like the Battle of the Somme.

> BASEL *shrugging in ignorance.*

World War I. A blood bath. Papers full of the most appalling reports. But the film footage—two silent minutes—shot by a lone cameraman—a long line of soldiers, heading up a hill, tiny shadows, silhouetted against the sky, to the top of the ridge… Over the edge, out of sight. Just a line… of shadows.

> *He parts his fingers, measuring scale.*

Suddenly humanity is reduced to— That small. Horrifying.

BASEL: And maybe… correct… somehow.

SKIP: Can't beat a close-up, though.

> *The faces are once again projected on their line.*

Let the faces tell the story.

> *Silence.* BASEL *withdraws slowly into the shadows.*

BASEL: When I think of my mother and sisters they are tiny shadows. Way out there, in the distance. Tiny shadows. Flickering. Too far away.

> *Silence.*

The projections flicker and fade. SKIP *is suddenly alone, at his beach house, staring at the moon.* AUGUSTUS *in spotlight, staring at the moon. He sings a lullaby.*

AUGUSTUS: I do not like blood. Especially my own. And this is the reason I am a pharmacist and not a surgeon. Less messy… for me… less money for my folks back home…

> He is a regular customer. Methadone. Off and on. Irregular. That morning he was panting manic. And early. Way too early.

> He said, *'Give me some of what you got!'*

> I said, *'What is it that you want?'*

He said, *'Just fucking give me some of what you've got! Or I'll give you some of what I've got!'*

A syringe full of blood. His, I assume. He is behind the counter with me, I step back, I am no fool. I let him take what he wants. He is stuffing pills into every pocket.

I say, *'Look. I know how hard it is for you. I know the kind of shit you're in. Things do not have to get this bad.'*

He stops. Laughs. As if I had just said the funniest thing. *'Don't patronise me, you lousy black cunt.'*

In his beach shack, SKIP *plucks a photo from the drying rope. Suddenly an explosion of gunfire and mortar shell. Pandemonium.* SKIP*'s memory of an event. Flickering projections of faces and smoke on the curtain/ blind behind them. His ears ring. Shell-shocked.*

SKIP: After the explosion, I lift myself up off the road… My ears ringing. Marketplace. Outside… Near… Jesus! Where are we? The town… What's the name of the town? Where are the bloody signs?

A cacophony of distant voices; unintelligible, distressed.

There's blood on my hands, but I'm not sure if it's mine, and—

SKIP *searches around him, dazed and attempting to find equilibrium, his ears still ringing.*

There's a woman. Lying in front of me. On the road. Through the smoke. Her skirt covering her face, as if she's asleep. Fast asleep. Dazed. Shell-shocked. Her underwear the colour of beetroot. I reach for my camera. And shoot. I'm on automatic. The click is comforting. Familiar. I move on. To the next. And the next. The next shot. That's what I do.

He begins to unravel.

There are children. Everywhere—on the road—so many children—

He holds back the emotion—sucks it in.

They never go away—the faces. The ones you don't shoot haunt you the longest. They stick. Under the skin. I step back. I walk away, and… then I remember. The music. The band. The dancing. He was dancing. Surrounded by children. Where is he? I can't see him—

Suddenly he panics.

BASEL! BASEL?!

Suddenly back at the beach house.

Halcyon Daze. Antiquated juvenilia abounds. NEVILLE *and* PATIENCE, *a music box in her hands; its melody tinny and tender. They listen; she captivated by it, he captivated by her.*

NEVILLE: Strange tune.

PATIENCE: I like it.

NEVILLE: Have no idea what it is. Which is frustrating.

PATIENCE: Some things are best left a mystery.

She closes the music box; the music ceases.

NEVILLE: Bingham's Toy Factory. Birmingham. Mass-produced, circa 1930. Cheap as chips, but not without charm. Particularly for Lilly Dean, of Chester. Later married and signed up for the ten pound passage to Australia. Passed from daughter to daughter. To the end of the line. Pre-renovation garage-sales cause people to turf out the most meaningful of objects. Sold it for a song, they did, handed it over, without batting even so much as a tear-soaked eyelid. Tragic.

PATIENCE: And yet they told you its story.

NEVILLE: Yes. They did.

PATIENCE: Now you are the keeper of its secrets.

NEVILLE: And its mystery.

Pause.

You're a mystery.

Pause.

There is so much I'd like to know.

PATIENCE: Nothing will come from telling.

Silence.

NEVILLE: Take it.
PATIENCE: What?
NEVILLE: It's yours.
PATIENCE: No.
NEVILLE: Yes.
PATIENCE: I couldn't—
NEVILLE: Why not?
PATIENCE: Because—
NEVILLE: I want you to have it. As a gift.
PATIENCE: For what?
NEVILLE: Nothing. That's what friends do.
PATIENCE: Friends. Yes. Thank you.
NEVILLE: You're welcome.

> *She opens it, the music plays.*

Night. Beach shack. SKIP *on mobile, his back to us.* BASEL, *arm bandaged, wanders in, unseen by him.*

SKIP: It's me. Skip. I—I just rang. I wanted to hear your voice and to tell you…

I just wanted to—I wonder if you saw my number and decided not to answer—or maybe you're busy and I don't know what we've come to and I'm—I just wanted to hear your voice…

> SKIP *turns and faces* BASEL. *Africa 2010. Late night/early morning.*

BASEL: I can't sleep.
SKIP: Join the club.
BASEL: Club? What club?
SKIP: Doesn't matter. How's the arm?
BASEL: It aches.
SKIP: You want a painkiller?

> BASEL *nods.* SKIP *gets up to for tablets and water.*

Here ya go. This'll do the trick.

> *Drugs are taken.*

BASEL: I do not like the dreams they bring.

SKIP: Comes with the territory. [*Indicating the tablets.*] May I?

BASEL: Yes.

SKIP: Cheers.

> SKIP *takes tablets.*

BASEL: Are you in pain?

SKIP: Nah. Just want to sleep.

> *Silence.*

BASEL: How do you do this?

SKIP: What?

BASEL: This. You run towards danger. You walk between bodies. You move from one photo to the next.

SKIP: That's my job. Without danger, I'm nothing, let's face it. I'm paid to chase it.

BASEL: Nothing touches you. Here.

> BASEL *pokes* SKIP *in the chest. Silence.*

SKIP: If I stopped, and let everything touch me, every dead eye I'm reflected in, I— If I let it touch me—

> *Pokes* BASEL *in his chest.*

I'm not a fucking machine... I just have thick armour.

> *Silence.*

I should take you back.

BASEL: Back? Where?

SKIP: The camp.

BASEL: The camp? No!

SKIP: You'll be safer.

BASEL: Please no—

SKIP: Look at you—

BASEL: I'm going to be okay—

SKIP: Are you?

BASEL: Yes!

SKIP: I'm not so sure.

BASEL: I am—not yet. Please.

SKIP: Not yet?

BASEL: Please… I…
SKIP: What are you waiting for?

> *Pause.*

Why did you want to come along? For the ride?
BASEL: I told you why.
SKIP: Yeah, yeah. And what else?

> *Pause.*

BASEL: I want to go back. To find them. Mama and my sisters. You can help me. Borders are safer with international press. Everyone knows this.

> *Pause.*

An exclusive.

> SKIP *cackles and shaking his head.*

SKIP: And what if there's nothing there?

> *Pause.*

What then?

> *Pause.*

Huh?

> *Pause.*

BASEL: Then you take me back.

> *Pause.*

SKIP: Win, win. Eh?

> *Pause.*

Beach shack, night. ALISON *enters. Silence.*

ALISON: This place stinks.

> *Pause.*

SKIP: Does it?
ALISON: Yes.

SKIP: Of what? My ammonia-scented piss?
ALISON: No. Fear.

> *Pause.*

I've smelt it before. Not on you, though. And not as strong.

> *Pause.*

What happened?
SKIP: What?
ALISON: Neville says you're not going back.

> *Pause.*

SKIP: I thought you'd be happy.
ALISON: I thought Africa was the love of your life.
SKIP: No. You are.

> ALISON *laughs, shaking her head.*

SKIP: Can you stay?

> *Pause.*

ALISON: Of course.

> *Pause.*

SKIP: I think I'm going mad.

> *Pause.*

ALISON: Photographers don't go mad. They just lose focus.

> SKIP *laughs… but it turns to sobs.* ALISON *watches.*

An explosion of music. SKIP*'s beach house. After lunch.* PATIENCE *and* AUGUSTUS *dance.* SKIP *follows* AUGUSTUS *and* PATIENCE *instructs* ALISON. *Much hilarity, all watched by* NEVILLE, *drink in hand. He skulls his wine, then pours another. The music ends and they collapse in their seats, exhausted.*

SKIP: Bloody fantastic—
PATIENCE: So hot now—
ALISON: Jeez—burnt my lunch off.

AUGUSTUS: A mere warm up—

SKIP: I feel like a swim. You feel like a swim?

Two conversations overlapping.

AUGUSTUS: No way, man.

ALISON: That dish was delicious, by the way.

AUGUSTUS: Too cold.

PATIENCE: Thank you.

SKIP: Nah. Invigorating.

ALISON: What was it?

SKIP: [*to* NEVILLE] You wanna come?

PATIENCE: Matura and Mahu.

NEVILLE: Where?

SKIP: A swim.

NEVILLE *shaking his head.*

PATIENCE: Standard Burundian meal.

AUGUSTUS: Arctic, man.

ALISON: Beef, was it?

PATIENCE: Yes.

ALISON: Yum. I love meat.

NEVILLE: You shouldn't swim—Drink, anyone?

PATIENCE: No. Thank you.

SKIP: Why not?

ALISON: [*drinking*] Thanks.

AUGUSTUS: [*drinking*] Thanks.

NEVILLE: You've just eaten. You'll cramp.

PATIENCE: It is nice to cook for other people.

SKIP: That is a total myth.

ALISON: Ya reckon? I hate it.

PATIENCE *and* ALISON *laugh.*

NEVILLE: No, it isn't.

SKIP: It is.

AUGUSTUS: Go swim, and find out.

NEVILLE: Aunty Iris always warned me.

SKIP: Misery guts!

ALISON: You made many friends?

PATIENCE: [*nodding*] Yes. I have many. Now.

NEVILLE: Do you?

PATIENCE: Yes. I do.

ALISON: [*awkward recovery*] Great!

SKIP: I've been dancing—

PATIENCE: [*to* ALISON] Burundian women. Like me.

SKIP: And I'm not cramping—

NEVILLE: Never swim on a full stomach—she said. Or you'll end up like my poor Ern.

ALISON: Is the Burundian community large here?

SKIP: Jesus.

PATIENCE: Yes. Big enough.

AUGUSTUS: Who?

SKIP: Great Uncle Ern. Married to Aunty Iris. Idiot of a man. Thought Hitler's Christian name was Ile.

> AUGUSTUS *and* SKIP *laugh.*

NEVILLE: He ate a full picnic lunch and then went swimming in the Murray, cramped and drowned.

SKIP: Nah—Uncle Ern drowned cause he was pissed.

NEVILLE: No, he didn't!

SKIP: He did! Dad told me. He was there. Some family thing. Uncle Ern wandered off, pissed as a newt, and fell in.

PATIENCE: Oh. Dear.

ALISON: Tragic.

NEVILLE: [*sullenly*] That's not the story Aunty Iris told.

SKIP: Yeah, well—she was a deluded old cow.

> NEVILLE *drains his glass.*

ALISON: You found work yet?

SKIP: Easy on the clutch there, Ern.

NEVILLE: What?

PATIENCE: Pardon?

> SKIP *mimes the drinking action.*

ALISON: Work. You found anything?

> NEVILLE *skulls his drink in defiance.* AUGUSTUS *shakes his head and clicks his tongue.*

PATIENCE: Yes, I have—

NEVILLE: Yes—she has—she's going to be working in my shop—

ALISON: Really!?

NEVILLE: Aren't you?

>*Pause.*

Aren't you?

PATIENCE: No. I'm not.

NEVILLE: Not?

AUGUSTUS: Anyone feel like a walk?

PATIENCE: I have a job at the hospital.

ALISON: Which one?

NEVILLE: Hospital? Since when?

AUGUSTUS: Anyone?

PATIENCE: St. Andrews.

ALISON: Nice. Central.

PATIENCE: I only found out yesterday.

SKIP: Had me appendix taken out there in eighty-one—

ALISON: And historically significant.

NEVILLE: Doing what?

PATIENCE: Cleaning.

ALISON: Good money?

PATIENCE: [*nodding*] Yes. I think so. It is good for me.

NEVILLE: Cleaning?

PATIENCE: Yes.

ALISON: Good hours?

PATIENCE: Yes. Enough.

NEVILLE: Cleaning?

>AUGUSTUS *groans.*

PATIENCE: Yes. Cleaning. And why not? I am good at it. [*To* ALISON] My friend, she will work with me. The same shifts. We can catch the trains together.

ALISON: That's fantastic.

NEVILLE: Why didn't you tell me?

PATIENCE: I'm sorry.

NEVILLE: I offered you a job, a perfectly good job in my shop—no cleaning required—

AUGUSTUS: Hey, man—come on—

NEVILLE: Why didn't you tell me?

PATIENCE: I'm sorry. Perhaps we should talk about this later.

NEVILLE: Right. Later. Yep.

ALISON: Neville.

NEVILLE: What!?

AUGUSTUS: Calm down, man—

NEVILLE: Fuck off.

SKIP: Hey—

AUGUSTUS: Okay.

> PATIENCE *stands, suddenly. Uncomfortable, ashamed, not knowing which way to go.*

PATIENCE: I think… I'll go for a walk… for a… time…

NEVILLE: I'll come—

PATIENCE: No! Alone—if you please…

> PATIENCE *hesitates before exiting. Silence.*

SKIP: Well done, Nev.

ALISON: Skip—

AUGUSTUS: What was all that about?

NEVILLE: Sorry.

SKIP: You're pissed.

NEVILLE: So are you.

SKIP: No; I'm naturally effusive. You fucked up, boyo.

> NEVILLE *covers his face, sways a little.*

NEVILLE: Yeah. Big time. Surprise.

> ALISON *advances to him and puts her arm around him, comforting.*

ALISON: What's going on?

> NEVILLE *sighs, shrugging her off and moves off.*

NEVILLE: Buggered if I know. As per fucking usual.

SKIP: Where are you going?

NEVILLE: A walk.

ALISON: I'll come—

NEVILLE: No.

SKIP: Don't you go in the water. Wouldn't want you to cramp and
drown.

NEVILLE: Piss off.

> NEVILLE *exits. Silence.* SKIP *sighs.*

AUGUSTUS: Tears before bedtime…

> *The light alters, slowly, each character silent and contemplative
> as the sun sets, their faces turned toward it.* ALISON *stands.*

ALISON: I'll clean up.

> *She exits followed by* SKIP. AUGUSTUS *looks out to sea.*

AUGUSTUS: The nurse said that she would sing to me, if that would
make me feel better. I said—why would I want that? She said—
Your face is very pale. I said—That's a first!… A joke… But she
didn't get it. Thank you—I said—but I will sing for myself.

I let them take my blood… Now it's all about waiting.

> SKIP *returns.*

AUGUSTUS: Man, you look like shit.

SKIP: You don't look so hot yourself, fatboy.

> AUGUSTUS *laughs.*

SKIP: You told me to fall apart. Read it and weep.

AUGUSTUS: I miss you.

SKIP: Jesus! Oprah moment!

AUGUSTUS: I do. I miss you. Miss this. Us. Like old times.

SKIP: Old times? Drinking in the Uni bar?

AUGUSTUS: We are older and wiser now.

SKIP: Are we? I wonder.

AUGUSTUS: Speak for yourself.

> *Silence.* ALISON *enters and kisses them both.*

ALISON: I'm going to bed.

> ALISON *exits.*

AUGUSTUS: How is she doing?

SKIP: Fine. I think.

AUGUSTUS: She must be missing him.

SKIP: Who?

AUGUSTUS: Her father.

Pause.

SKIP: Missing him?

Pause.

AUGUSTUS: You don't know?

AUGUSTUS *sighs.*

SKIP: Know what?

AUGUSTUS: Jesus Christ. What kind of weird dance are you two on?

The Beach. Sunset. After the lunch. NEVILLE *is drunk.* PATIENCE *is angry.*

NEVILLE: I'm sorry.

PATIENCE: Yes. As am I.

Silence.

NEVILLE: I can't help it. I just—like to know—

PATIENCE: [*anger rising*] Everything. Yes, I know! But I do not *want* you to know *everything*. I do not want *anyone* to know *every*thing. Do I know everything about you? Or your brother? Or Alison?

NEVILLE: What do you want to know? Ask and I'll tell you. Anything.

PATIENCE: I do not want to know!

Pause.

NEVILLE: I embarrassed you.

PATIENCE: Yes. You did. But more so yourself.

NEVILLE: I'm sorry.

PATIENCE: Why do you drink so much? I do not like you as this man.

NEVILLE: I'm sorry.

PATIENCE: Please stop saying that word.

NEVILLE: I'm… penitent.

PATIENCE: You do not own me.

Pause.

NEVILLE: No. I don't.

PATIENCE: I think it best if we walk away from each other as soon as we can.

SKIP: What?

PATIENCE: Shake hands and wish each other good luck.

NEVILLE: No—

PATIENCE: You are a very nice man. And I am very thankful for your friendship and kindness—

SKIP: Kindness?

PATIENCE: But I cannot give you what you want.

NEVILLE: What I want?

PATIENCE: Yes.

NEVILLE: And what would that be?

PATIENCE: Everything. Too much.

Pause.

NEVILLE: [*crestfallen*] Right.

PATIENCE: You are offended now.

NEVILLE: No. No.

PATIENCE: Yes. Yes.

NEVILLE: What do you want me to do?

PATIENCE: You cannot make this decision yourself?

NEVILLE: Everything I decide to do always seems to be wrong,

Pause.

PATIENCE: You sober up.

NEVILLE: I sober up.

PATIENCE: We get in the car. You drive me back.

NEVILLE: I drive her back. In silence.

PATIENCE: You park the car outside my apartment.

NEVILLE: It is dark. Too dark.

PATIENCE: And we say goodbye.

NEVILLE: She does not meet my eyes… What have I done?…

PATIENCE: We shake hands.

NEVILLE: I hold on for too long. She pulls away.

PATIENCE: And wish each other well.

NEVILLE: And now what?

Pause.

PATIENCE: I walk away. To my mop. You drive away. To your shop.

Pause.

NEVILLE: And that's it?

PATIENCE: Yes. That's it.

Late at night. Australia. SKIP *is drinking heavily, going through photos on his digital camera and they are projected behind him. They are all of an abandoned, war-damaged house in Northwestern Liberia.* BASEL *enters. He is emotional.*

BASEL: Nothing. There is nothing.

Pause.

There is no-one.

Pause.

SKIP: It was always a possibility. You knew that.

Silence.

BASEL: This is where our home was. Here. Right here. This is the kitchen where Mama cooked.

Music. BASEL *moves through a tour of the house.* SKIP *photographs.*

And through here. My room. And my sisters'.

SKIP *begins shooting him as he moves through the invisible house.*

BASEL: There was a window, there. And when you laid down on the bed, you could see Cousin Poni's house. You could see the swing in her back yard. And I'd see Mama—walking back from the well. At sunrise… coming up the road—

BASEL *cries, uncontrollably; an outpouring of grief.* SKIP *continues to shoot.*

[*Sobbing*] Mama!

BASEL *falls to his knees.* SKIP *keeps shooting. It is noticed by* BASEL. *His grief turns to rage, and he turns on* SKIP.

BASEL *physically assaults* SKIP. *An ugly and violent scuffle.* BASEL *punches* SKIP *and he falls to the ground.*

SKIP: Shit!

BASEL: What are you doing?! Huh! Cut that shit out!

SKIP: Okay, okay!

BASEL: What are you doing?! You think I want this in my face?

SKIP: I'm sorry.

BASEL: I am not one of your stories!

SKIP: Yes, you are! You signed on for that the moment you opened your fucking mouth back at the camp! You chose me! Win, win! That's what it means. You scratch my back. I scratch yours.

> SKIP *waves his hand dismissively, in a rage.* ALISON *enters unseen.*

Get in the fucking car! I'm taking you back!

> SKIP *turns around in circles, in a fury.* BASEL *disappears. Suddenly the beach house.*

ALISON: What are you doing?

SKIP: Fucking ridiculous idea! Fucking party! I don't need other people's shit!

ALISON: It was your idea.

SKIP: How did he die? Your father.

> *Pause.*

ALISON: Stroke. A big one.

SKIP: Bummer. I'm sorry.

> *Pause.*

ALISON: So am I...

SKIP: When were you intending to tell me?

ALISON: I was waiting. For the right moment.

SKIP: The *right moment*?

ALISON: That's what life is with you! It's never the right moment!

SKIP: *This is not about me!*

ALISON: *Everything is about you!* And the fucking distance. Even when you're here, now—there's this fucking continent between us.

> *Pause.*

SKIP: He was your father!

ALISON: You barely knew him.

SKIP: *He was your father!* Jesus Christ! Is there anything else you're not telling me? Any other secrets you're keeping?

ALISON: Secrets?! I'm not the one hiding away from the world, falling apart! I'm not the one with blood soaked pictures covering my floor, am I?

>   *Pause.*

I wonder, when you're not here, how much of you will come back. How much will you have left behind. And then I think—were you ever really here? Have I ever met all of you? I catch my breath, when I think of it. What I've let myself in for. What I've given up. For you. For this.

SKIP: This?

ALISON: *Yes! This!* Whatever *this* is!

SKIP: I warned you.

>   *An impasse. A lengthy silence.*

ALISON: Yes. You did.

>   ALISON *exits.*

◆   ◆   ◆   ◆

2 am in the morning. AUGUSTUS.

AUGUSTUS: I wake in a cold sweat in the early hours. I cannot sleep. I am on a farm on the outskirts of Endouli, Western Cape, South Africa. My brother and I stand at the edge of a dry field, a haze of dust stirred by cattle hangs like a cloud before us. My twelfth birthday. A hot day. I feel the trickle of sweat that runs in a straight line between my shoulders. Then we run, my little brother and I, across the fields, to the edges, to our hiding spot. Beneath towering pampas, crickets ringing in song. I hold up a cigarette, stolen from Grandfather, between my fingers, flashing white teeth in a devilish smile at my little brother. I strike a match. It hisses into a tiny flame, and I choke on the first gasp. I double over, my head spinning. And the match drops from my fingers.

The back wall burns.

The grass explodes into a wall of flame. Perhaps if we pee on it, my brother says, his voice like a squealing pig. I run, dragging my brother, every muscle straining, towards home, the fire chasing us, unrolling like a carpet, a wave of flame and smoke. I do not turn to look. I feel the heat at my back, hear the cattle screaming, stampeding. And see them—my family, watching, hearing it all burn. Our life, our inheritance. There is nothing, nothing they can do.

Music.

There is no punishment. No beatings. No harsh words. Only silence. And eyes that avoid mine. The realisation that there are some things that can never be undone. Things that do not heal with time. Things that sit within you forever, like a rock, a hot coal. The fear, hot and fast. Forever at your back.

Music—fluid. SKIP *and* BASEL. ALISON, *at a distance, listening.*

SKIP: The Oasis Hotel. In the middle of nowhere.

BASEL: Why have we stopped?

SKIP: Sleep.

BASEL: I'm not tired.

SKIP: Maybe they have an all night buffet. All you can eat.

BASEL: I'm not hungry.

SKIP: Gotta give you some pleasure. It is called the Oasis, after all.

    Silence.

I'm sorry. That you didn't find what you wanted to.

    Pause.

BASEL: I'm sorry. For hitting you.

    SKIP *shrugging.*

SKIP: There are times, when I'm not invisible…

    Water is reflected on all surfaces.

BASEL: *Oh my god!*

> SKIP *laughs.*

ALISON: What?

SKIP: A swimming pool. It had a bloody swimming pool.

BASEL: I want to swim. Now.

SKIP: No, mate. Not now. It's late. I'm stuffed. I want to sleep.

BASEL: When then?

SKIP: In the morning. After breakfast.

BASEL: You said you should never swim on a full stomach.

> SKIP *laughs.*

SKIP: Okay, before breakfast. At dawn. Wake me. Come on. Let's get some sleep.

> SKIP *goes to leave, but* BASEL *does not follow.*

BASEL: I'm not tired. I just want to sit here for a moment longer.

SKIP: Just a moment longer… then sleep.

> BASEL *nodding.* SKIP *turns to leave.*

And I left him. Poolside. I left him. I went to my room. And climbed into bed. I left him.

> *Lights alter and music halts.* BASEL *lies on his back, lifeless.* SKIP *snaps; overcome by grief. He crouches over* BASEL *and attempts to revive him.*

No, no, no—Jesus Christ—come on—come, come on—please— *No, no no—Jesus—Come on! I can't save him. I can't save him! Come on! Come on!*

> *He picks up* BASEL *in an embrace, rocking him back and forth, completely lost in his grief. He cries freely.*

A montage. Music. Lives overlapping.

NEVILLE *sits in his shop, eating sandwiches from the antiquated lunchbox. Will, a projection, sits near him, folding a paper aeroplane on his lap. He launches it into the air, and* NEVILLE *follows its trajectory.*

It flies above the head of PATIENCE, *who walks down a long hospital corridor.*

SKIP *flicks through images on his laptop; an endless loop.*

AUGUSTUS *exits a doctor's room in the hospital, dazed and pale. He wanders past* PATIENCE, *at a distance. She sees him, and follows.*

Will exits, watched after by NEVILLE, *who closes his lunchbox, and follows him off, passing* PATIENCE.

SKIP *closes his laptop with a snap.*

A hospital. PATIENCE *is behind* AUGUSTUS.

PATIENCE: Augustus?

AUGUSTUS *turns to face her, his face a blank mask. A beat.*

It's me. Patience.
AUGUSTUS: Hello.

Pause.

PATIENCE: Are you alright?
AUGUSTUS: Yes. I—I need—
PATIENCE: What? What do you need?

He pulls car keys from his pocket.

AUGUSTUS: Get home—

AUGUSTUS *crouches, suddenly, overtaken by shock and nausea.*

[*An exhalation*] Jesus.
PATIENCE: Would you like me to call for someone?
AUGUSTUS: No! No. I'm just—I've just had—I'm okay. Just let me—
Let me catch my breath.
PATIENCE: Okay.

PATIENCE *looks around to see if anyone of assistance is nearby.*

AUGUSTUS: You work here?
PATIENCE: Yes.

AUGUSTUS: It has been a long time since I saw you last.
PATIENCE: Yes.
AUGUSTUS: The lunch. At the beach.
PATIENCE: Yes. We danced.

    AUGUSTUS *stands.*

AUGUSTUS: That's right. We did.
PATIENCE: Would you like a chair?
AUGUSTUS: No. Thank you.
PATIENCE: I think you should. Sit down. For a time.
AUGUSTUS: Do you?
PATIENCE: Yes.
AUGUSTUS: Where?
PATIENCE: Here. Just for a moment. Please.

    AUGUSTUS *sits, for her benefit rather than his.*

That's better, I think.
AUGUSTUS: Much. Thank you.

    Pause.

PATIENCE: So… how have you been?
AUGUSTUS: Me? Oh, I'm fantastic.
PATIENCE: Yes?
AUGUSTUS: Yes. Going from strength to strength, you know.

    Pause.

Life's grand for all. At the moment.

    Silence. PATIENCE *slowly moves and sits beside him. Embraces him. It's awkward, but it's what he needs.*

ALISON: She rings me. Suddenly needy. Utterly distressed. Saying she can't take it anymore. *'Take what, Mum?'*

    She says, 'The silence. When are you coming next? I've made lemon butter.' It's never an open invitation but a summons, immediate and rigid. The hardest part about losing my father is the fact I've lost her too. Without him, she's set hard. In all her brittle and thorny glory—unrelieved by him. Just one half of the team. I gird my loins. I clench before going into battle. Suck it in, glance at my watch and silently schedule departure time. And—

Pause.

She's standing in the kitchen. I see her through the back door, her back to me, facing the empty seat.

Pause.

She's... so *small*. And frail. And old. My Mum is an old woman. And she's alone. The house swims around her like cathedral. And I'm all she's got.

Pause.

I enter. Silently. She doesn't turn. I sit between her and the emptiness. I think of the years. All their years. Spent. Together. And now nothing. I think of the future—the emptiness that is coming for me. One day. And I want to know. I want her to tell me. Because I don't know anymore. *'Is it worth it? Mum? Is it worth it?'*

Silence.

She looks at me through years too numerous to judge. And says, suddenly present, *'What have you done to your hair?'*

Halcyon Daze. NEVILLE *and* SKIP. *A wrapped present between them. A projected image of Will sits near him, waiting, legs swinging above the floor.* SKIP *hands* NEVILLE *a framed picture of a smiling child from an unspecified African nation.*

NEVILLE: It's beautiful. Thanks.

SKIP: Pleasure. One more for the collection.

NEVILLE: I don't want you to go.

SKIP: I'll be back.

NEVILLE: Yeah, I know. I just—I want to keep hold of—I'm so scared of losing things. People—I hold on too tight.

SKIP: No, you don't.

NEVILLE: Yes. I do. Which is why I'm where I am. Surrounded by all this. Stuff. A lonely tragic balding smothering man.

SKIP: You are not balding.

>NEVILLE *laughs. They embrace.*

ONWARD and upward, mate. Something better just around the corner.
NEVILLE: Yeah. Sure. Send me a postcard.
SKIP: Will do.
NEVILLE: Tacky. Make sure it's tacky.
SKIP: I'll do my best. Give my love to Will.
NEVILLE: Yep. Be safe.

>SKIP *turns and exits into shadows.* NEVILLE *turns back into the shop, to the wrapped present. He holds it up, speaks to the projection of Will.*

BIRTHDAY present. Fifties tin robot. One owner. Mint condition. Cost an arm and a leg. But worth it. Flashing lights, chrome, and a growl to wake the dead. You'll love it.

>*Projection of Will fades, leaving him alone.*

>*The shop door bell rings with an unseen customer. He pulls himself together.*

ONWARD and upward.

The roar of jet engines. An airport departure lounge. SKIP, *set for travel, resigned to the return, and* ALISON *wait silently. Bodies criss-cross the space, but* SKIP *and* ALISON *do not notice them—each in their own world.*

SKIP: You should have just dropped me and gone. Instead of waiting around.
ALISON: No. I'm used to waiting. I'm good at it.

>*Silence.* ALISON *looks at her watch.*

SKIP: You're going to be late for work.
ALISON: Screw 'em.

>*Silence.* SKIP *takes her hand.*

SKIP: The last time.

ALISON: Uh huh.

SKIP: I mean it.

ALISON: Yep.

SKIP: You don't believe me?

Silence.

I promise.

ALISON *laughs derisively, shaking her head.*

ALISON: Don't. This scene will go on, repeated over and over again. Skip and Alison in departure lounge. Skip returns to Africa to chase danger. Alison stays home and hopes he comes back in one piece. Over and over. Until you're too old and frail to lift a camera, or you're gunned down by Ugandan rebels—or you just disappear into a cloud of dust.

Silence. He hugs her, suddenly and passionately.

SKIP: I'm stuck.

Then he releases her and steps back.

I love you.

ALISON: Der! Tell me something I don't know!

Silence.

SKIP: Go.

Silence. ALISON *exits. A jet engine roars overhead.*

Music—African—an anthem. Lights. Australia. A gathering— memorial. Entire cast.

NEVILLE: When we were kids, all my brother really wanted to be was Chuck Berry. And Elvis Presley. And Eric Clapton. Freddie Mercury. Roger Daltry. Lou Reed. Bryan Ferry. And even—God forbid—for a brief time—in an adolescent lapse of taste—Lionel Richie. The music might've changed but the dance steps didn't. Always his best step forward. Focussed. Obsessed in his plan.

SKIP: All I want—

NEVILLE: He said. All I want—

SKIP: Is to be famous … cool … With a string of hit songs …

NEVILLE: Naturally, as devoted and dopey brothers do, I followed him. Blindly. Breathlessly. Always in awe of him. In his quest. In spite of possessing no musical ability whatsoever. Neither of us.

WHILST every other boy in our street played cricket in the streets, we became The Millers—Unplugged—singers—songwriters.

SONGS—

SONGS with names like: *Rubik's Cube Fever*, *I'm in Love with Mr Whippy's Sister* and *I Just Wanna Rent Jana Wendt*

WE were on our way … Our mother, however—practical no-crap Yank that she was—was less encouraging. And for one good, honest, no-crap reason: we were terrible.

[*AS Mom*] Ya wanna be famous, then do what your good at. Don't sing … We took her advice. We always did. The Millers disbanded and in a fit of bruised ego all lyrics were burnt at the stake of the backyard barbecue. A silent, sausage-scented occasion. The hit songs were forgotten.

A change of mood. The projections change to SKIP*'s photographs—faces of Africa. Music.*

BUT in his pictures—in the faces—the unblinking eyes—in the curve of the lips—even the ones that take your breath away in horror—sadness—there is music. A different sound within every frame. Every story told without words. Music. That rumbles beneath my feet, and rises.

THAT took me by surprise at first. Took my breath away. That my brother did this—captured this—stood so close to this.

THESE are his hit songs.

Every wall shimmers with the faces of SKIP*'s work. A choir sings, soaring, their image projected on every surface. Lights fade.*

THE END